Window to the World

*Extraordinary Stories from a
Century of Overseas Mission
1900-2000*

Tina Block Ediger, writer and compiler

FAITH & LIFE
PRESS
Newton, Kansas
Winnipeg, Manitoba

Window to the World
Extraordinary Stories from a Century of Overseas Mission
1900-2000

Copyright © 1999 by Commission on Overseas Mission, General
Conference Mennonite Church, Newton, Kansas 67114-00347

Cooperatively published by the Commission on Overseas
Mission of the General Conference Mennonite Church, and
Faith & Life Press. COM and FLP are both located at:
722 Main Street, P.O. Box 347, Newton Kansas 67114-0347
and
600 Shaftesbury Boulevard, Winnipeg, Manitoba R3P 0M4

Printed in the United States of America.

ISBN 0-87303-396-5

Compiled by Tina Block Ediger; editorial services by Faith &
Life Press; cover and interior design by John Hiebert; printed
by Mennonite Press, Inc. Cover photos by Ron Flaming.

Dedication

- to all whose stories are told in these pages;

- to workers who shared their gifts in service through the General Conference Mennonite Church overseas mission program (see page 147);

- to congregations and individuals who prayed and gave money;

- to the parents and grandparents who blessed their children as they went forth;

- to board/commission members and office staff who have served these 100 years; and

- to Mennonite leaders who had a passion for missions and who felt God leading missions into new paths of partnership.

Table of Contents

Foreword

Mission has been at the heart of the Christian church since Pentecost. It has also been a driving force in the General Conference Mennonite Church since its founding in 1860, as people have shared the life-changing gospel of Jesus Christ with others. The General Conference became involved in cross-cultural mission in other nations in 1900. By God's grace and the sacrificial efforts of hundreds of people of many backgrounds, the Holy Spirit has moved in amazing ways.

In 1991 Erwin Rempel, then executive secretary of the General Conference Commission on Overseas Mission (COM), recognized that COM's 100th anniversary was less than a decade away. He initiated discussion about whether COM might publish a book marking this century of international ministry. The commission agreed, and dreaming began.

The dream took shape. Staff, a committee, and eventually a compiler/writer expanded the dream. We wanted something that people of all ages could enjoy and be inspired by as they visited its pages. We envisioned a coffee-table book of stories and pictures of international people whose lives have been touched by General Conference mission endeavors. We wanted people to catch glimpses of God at work in the lives of Christian sisters and brothers with whom we have partnered.

This book is the fruit of all this dreaming and work. I heartily commend Tina Block Ediger and COM for offering this history of mission making a difference, a history of changes and realignments as we moved from pioneering mission to partnerships with overseas churches. It is intriguing to read in this book the words of my good friend, Milka Rindzinski from Uruguay: "The momentum for God in my life has never left." So also, the "momentum for God" in mission continues. Let us praise God as we read the stories of these 100 years.

—Glendon Klaassen
COM Executive Secretary, 1994-1998
COM Latin America Secretary, 1981-1996
COM Missionary in Colombia, 1959-1977

Acknowledgements

In addition to those who submitted their stories, my special thanks go to Doreen Harms, Esther Rinner, and Luella Stahly all of North Newton, who typed them; to my sister J. Martha Epp from Ontario who helped me for a month; to Commission On Overseas Mission staff, particularly Nancy Funk, without whose help this book could not have been written; to my family and friends who encouraged me along the way; to the editorial committee members who made such helpful suggestions: Lois Friesen, James Juhnke, Robert Kreider, Paul Schrag, Muriel Thiessen Stackley, and Jeannie Zehr; and to the editorial staff of Faith & Life Press. It was a joy to work with these brothers and sisters on this assignment.

—*Tina Block Ediger*

Tina Block Ediger, a native of Steinbach, Manitoba, served on staff with the Commission on Overseas Mission in Newton, Kansas, from 1955 to 1981. Those years included a term of service in India from 1961 to 1963, and 11 years as Secretary of Mission Communications. From 1986 to 1996, she worked in public relations with Prairie View, a regional mental health center in Newton. With her late spouse Elmer Ediger, she has two step-daughters, a stepson, and six grandchildren. She lives in North Newton, where she gardens, entertains, and writes family history.

bbreviations

AIMM	Africa Inter-Mennonite Mission
CEM	Evangelical Mennonite Church of Congo
CHM	Commission on Home Ministries
CIM	Council of International Ministries
CMC	Conference of Mennonites in Canada
CMCo	Congo Mennonite Church, earlier known as Mennonite Church of Congo
COM	Commission on Overseas Mission
CUMA	Committee for United Anabaptist Mission
EMM	Eastern Mennonite Missions
FOMCIT	Fellowship of Mennonite Churches in Taiwan
GCMC or GC	General Conference Mennonite Church
MAF	Mission Aviation Fellowship
MBM	Mennonite Board of Missions
MCC	Mennonite Central Committee
MLA	Mennonite Library and Archives
TEE	Theological Education by Extension

Introduction

A South African proverb says, "If you inherit land, you have to farm it. If you inherit a story, you have to tell it." In a century of General Conference Mennonite Church overseas mission, we have inherited many stories of God's faithfulness and blessing. This collection is a way to pass on that precious heritage—a tribute to all who served overseas, whose lives touched others in order that they, too, might serve. It is a celebration of God at work in the lives of ordinary people.

Since the first missionaries landed in Bombay, India, in 1900, more than 900 others have served with General Conference missions in 30 countries. In this book you will learn about some of them, usually through the eyes of those they served, as well as their stories. As you read, I hope you will catch a glimpse of how God's interactions with people transform lives and communities in every culture, including the lives of missionaries *and* those who provided financial and prayer support. I hope you will see how God has been weaving Mennonite churches around the world into a beautiful tapestry, each race and culture adding its own vibrant colors and stories of faithfulness.

The stories are grouped around major phases of our mission history. First there was the "colonial" era in India, China, Congo, and Paraguay. Over the years, we learned what it meant to turn over leader-

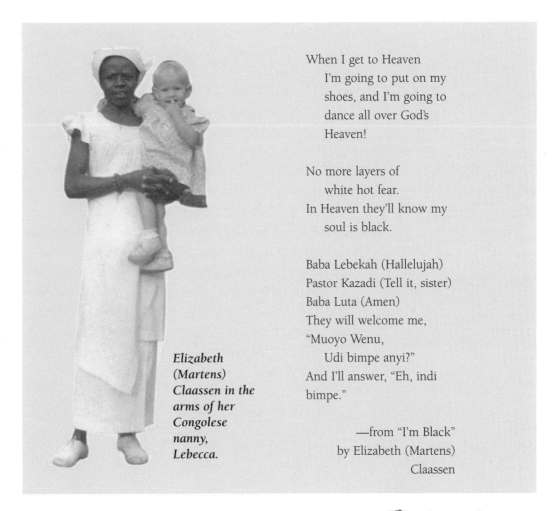

Elizabeth (Martens) Claassen in the arms of her Congolese nanny, Lebecca.

When I get to Heaven
   I'm going to put on my
   shoes, and I'm going to
   dance all over God's
   Heaven!

No more layers of
   white hot fear.
In Heaven they'll know my
   soul is black.

Baba Lebekah (Hallelujah)
Pastor Kazadi (Tell it, sister)
Baba Luta (Amen)
They will welcome me,
"Muoyo Wenu,
   Udi bimpe anyi?"
And I'll answer, "Eh, indi
bimpe."

      —from "I'm Black"
      by Elizabeth (Martens)
      Claassen

ship, keys, and dollars to the growing national churches in those countries, and to work in partnership with them.

The next phase, after World War II, was one of expansion as we entered more countries to share the gospel, plant churches, and meet human needs through ministries of education and health. In contrast to the "colonial" era, missionaries had the mandate to turn over the leadership of the church to the local people as soon as was possible.

Partnerships with other Mennonite mission agencies and established churches overseas since 1980 mark the third phase. That phase continues, even as we explore new kinds of ventures in international missions.

To obtain these stories, I wrote to Commission on Overseas Mission workers, both past and present, and to the adult children of earlier missionaries. I invited them to tell me of the people who made a difference in the lives of the churches and communities where they lived and served. My excitement rose with the first response, which came from Elizabeth (Martens) Claassen, the daughter of Elvina (Neufeld) and Rudy Martens. She wrote a

poem in honor of and dedicated to Lebecca, the woman who cared for her while her mother, a medical doctor, worked in a hospital in Congo. Elizabeth's daughter, Rebecca, is named after her.

Other stories soon followed—fascinating accounts of extraordinary ordinary people whose lives gave me a window to the poor, the seeking, the marginal, the hurting—and to the difference the gospel made in their lives. I want to thank those who submitted stories. I also express my regrets for not having been able to include all of them. Stories not included in this book are available from the Commission on Overseas Mission office for a small fee (722 Main, P.O. Box 347, Newton, KS 67114; phone: 316 283-5100).

Many of these stories have been condensed or edited to fit the format of the book. I invite you, however, to listen to the variety of voices among the storytellers. Read them aloud; tell them to children. Use them as a resource in your home and congregation. May they inspire you to tell your own stories of faith, mission, and service.

—*Tina Block Ediger*

Chapter 1

Soup, Soap, and Salvation

MISSIONS FOUNDED IN THE COLONIAL ERA

India, China, Congo, Paraguay

The turn of the last century was a heady time for mission-minded Mennonites in North America. Since 1880 the General Conference Mennonite Church had been reaching across cultural boundaries to share the gospel with Native Americans in Oklahoma. Now, new opportunities were beckoning from across the ocean. The colonization of African and Asian countries by European powers had opened the way for missionaries to establish ministries of evangelism, health, and education among many people of many cultures. For General Conference Mennonites, the famine in India at the end of the nineteenth century was the entry point for a mission of compassion beyond North America. Other countries, notably China, Congo, and Paraguay, followed.

Most mission leaders today recognize that the style of missions dating before World War II tended to be paternalistic, and too often seemed to reflect the political ambitions of the colonial powers. Some methods and vocabulary of those days would be embarassing today. However, as the stories here point out, God's Word nonetheless took root, and lives were transformed. Missionaries often left behind not only institutions that brought learning and healing to many, but personal legacies of faithfulness and love.

India

With tearful farewells and the assurance of God's abiding presence, the General Conference Mennonite Church sent its first workers to India in 1900. Four young and eager missionaries, P.A. and Elizabeth (Dickman) Penner from Mountain Lake, Minnesota, and John F. and Susanna (Hirschler) Kroeker from Russia and Germany, arrived in Bombay on December 9, 1900. After surveying the state of Madhya Pradesh, they began ministries in Champa and Janjgir, not far from Dhamtari, where the Mennonite Church had established its mission.

Joining the Penners and Kroekers in 1906 were Peter J. and Agnes (Harder) Wiens, and Annie C. Funk. Peter W. and

"They (Helen E. Nickel and Augusta Schmidt) were so capable and took such personal interest in us girls that we came to love them as our own mothers. They were great, yet so simple and humble. We shall ever remain thankful to them for their love and guidance."
— *Dr. Theresa Patil, former Funk Memorial School student, India*

P. A. Penner in thought.

1

Peter A. and Elizabeth (Dickman) Penner, ca. 1900.

John F. and Susanna (Hirschler) Kroeker, ca. 1900.

Mathilde (Ensz) Penner arrived in 1908. Between 1909 and 1948, 53 more workers were added to the missionary family in India. In all, 126 missionaries served in that country from 1900 to 1998.

Early in his missionary career, P.A. Penner coined the phrase "soup, soap, and salvation," which describes the General Conference's philosophy of missions from the beginning—meeting the needs of the total human being: body, mind, and spirit. Besides schools, clinics, and hospitals, one of strengths of the work in India was village evangelism among the very poor. Evangelism gave birth to the Bharatiya General Conference Mennonite Church in 1912, with major centers in Champa, Janjgir, Jagdeeshpur, Mauhadih, and surrounding villages.

By the early 1970s the time had come for missionaries to relinquish their leadership of the Bharatiya General Conference Mennonite Church to the Indian Christians. Much of this transition was hastened by changing laws which affected missionaries in India. Visas were seldom granted or renewed, forcing some missionaries to leave on short notice. Missions scrambled to turn leadership and assets over to the Indian churches. The Commission on Overseas Mission's Goals, Priorities, and Strategy Study in 1972 was part of that movement, mandating rapid change. Inevitably, as with most missions, the changes brought stress, misunderstanding, and conflict, both in the mission and the church.

However, the work begun in faith by missionaries, and funded by COM, continued as the church bore its own burdens and stood on its own feet. When the General Conference Mennonite mission in India officially dissolved in 1989, COM created endowments to partially fund medical, educational, and evangelistic ministries. COM continues to provide some annual grants, especially for capital expenditures to Mennonite-operated schools and hospitals. It also supports short-term teachers on the faculty of Union Biblical Seminary in Pune.

The absence of foreign mission workers throughout India gave birth to indigenous missionary movements. In 1998 it was reported by Jai Prakash

India missionary family ca. 1911. Back: Peter J. and Agnes (Harder) Wiens, Peter A. Penner, P. W. and Mathilde (Ensz) Penner. Middle: Annie C. Funk, Martha (Richert) Penner. Front: Anna Braun, Lulu (Johnson) and Cornelius Suckau.

W.F. Unruh album, MLA

The first graduates of the Bible school in about 1933 in front of the Janjgir church in India with missionary William F. Unruh, its founder.

Agramati and Samson Walter, from Mahaudih, India, were outstanding leaders in education and the church. Their seven sons value the heritage they passed on to them. (Photo taken in 1959.)

Rod Hemley, 1968

Dr. Arthur Thiessen, surgeon, exams the formerly paralyzed hand of a leprosy patient at Bethesda Leprosy Homes and Hospital in Champa, India.

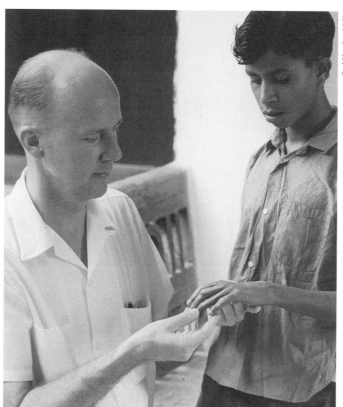

4

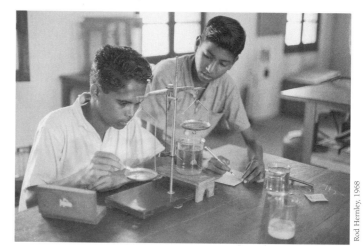

Rod Hemley, 1968

Students in the science laboratory at Jansen Memorial Higher Secondary School (JMS) in India.

India Missionary Conference in Korba in 1928. Missionaries wore pith helmets to protect themselves from the sun even before the dangers of its rays were fully known.

W.F. Unruh Album, MLA

Masih, a member of the Bharatiya General Conference Mennonite Church, that 12,000 to 15,000 Indian missionaries were reaching across language and cultural barriers, and that about 1.2 million people were brought to Christ every year. Although the Bharatiya General Conference

Mennonite Churches have not yet supported overseas missionaries, many of its dedicated young people are serving the Lord across cultural and linguistic borders in their country. Christianity is on the move in India.

"These missionaries (the P.A. Penners) had no beds, no tables, no well drinking water. They lived in tents for some time and bore the deprivations of pioneer life with courage and fortitude."
—*Trophenia Bai Banwan, India*

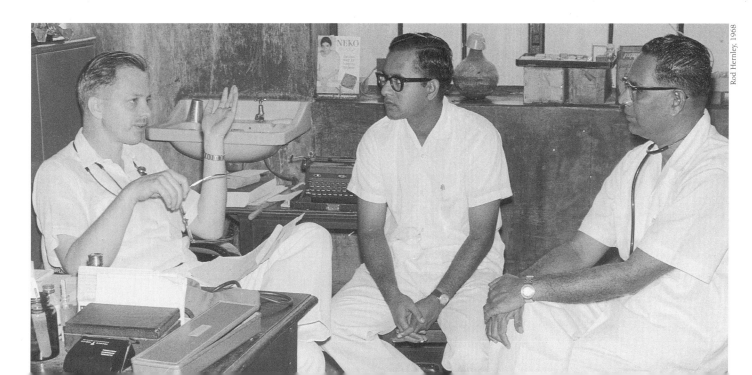

Rod Hernley, 1968

Missionary Dr. Joseph J. Duerksen in consultation with Drs. Cornelius Walter and T. Mathai at the Champa Christian Hospital.

5

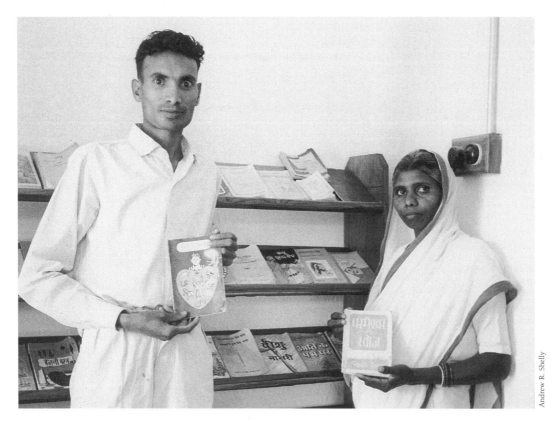

Ibrahim Nand and Pushpalata John care for the spiritual needs of the patients at Sewa Bhawan Hospital, Jagdeeshpur, India, 1966.

Andrew R. Shelly

". . . preparing human resources is the best investment of the church and mission because it gives dignity to the Lord's work."
—*Shekhar Singh, GC faculty at Union Biblical Seminary, Pune, India*

Professors Premanand and Rachel Sonwani Bagh and children represent the Bharatiya GC Mennonite Church of India at the Allahabad Biblical Seminary.

Premanand Bagh, C.S.R. Gier, Nathan R. Sona and Shautkuman Nunjam, members of the City Mennonite Ministries in Bhopal, India, in 1988.

6

China

Henry J. and Maria (Miller) Brown both felt a call to missionary service even before they knew each other. They married, and in 1909 sailed for China independent of the General Conference Mennonite Church. In southern Hopei province, they established an evangelistic and church planting ministry, and the work grew. Before long, they needed help. In 1914 the Browns asked the General Conference mission board to take responsibility for the Mennonite mission work in this region, which had a population of about two million. With missionary candidates in the United States waiting to respond to this need, the mission board accepted the challenge. New workers arrived, and more churches, schools, and a hospital were built.

Under the leadership of E.G. and Hazel (Dester) Kaufman, education in China became a priority. By 1926 the mission had erected some 60 schools. People were also in need of medical care. With the arrival of Dr. A.M. and Marie (Wollman) Lohrentz, nurses Frieda Sprunger and Elizabeth Goertz, and Dr. C.L. and Lelia (Roth) Pannabecker, the sick were treated. In 1926, medical work included a school of nursing. Chinese doctors and nurses were engaged. By 1940 the group had treated about 30,000 outpatients and over 1,000 inpatients.

Henry J. and Maria (Miller) Brown, the first General Conference missionaries in China, with their children (l–r) Linda, Jessie, and Roland, around 1927.

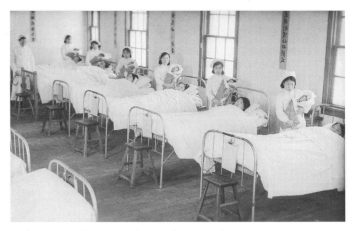

Hospital ward in Kai Chow, China, in the 1920s.

Two tents were set up in well-populated areas and left up for seven to 10 days. It took two to three years to cover the General Conference's large area in China.

Mr. and Mrs. Liu Ching Hsuan, evangelist and first pastor at Kai Chow, China.

Mr. and Mrs. Liu, evangelist and Bible woman.

Missionary S.F. Pannabecker, who arrived in China in 1923, reported that as the church grew and matured, problems also arose. In 1927 a civil war forced most missionaries to evacuate, leaving only a few to carry on the work. To add to the stress, famine conditions prevailed in that part of China.

The Chinese Church Conference came into being in 1936, when the mission in China celebrated its 25th anniversary. A few years later the mission organization was replaced by a general committee, composed mainly of Chinese and responsible to the conference. In 1942 the mission signed all mission properties over to the Chinese. Within 40 years of the missionaries' arrival, the church was a growing responsible body, with trained people in charge of every institution.

Mao Tse Tung's Communist revolution disrupted communication suddenly, and mission work was terminated. The hospitals and schools were

nationalized. When the last General Conference Mennonite missionaries left China in 1951, the church ran six mission stations, 24 congregations, a hospital, a school of nursing, several elementary schools, a high school, and a Bible school.

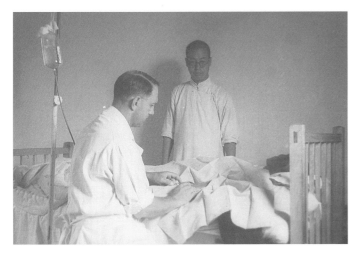

Dr. C. L. Pannabecker and a Chinese male nurse care for a patient.

World War II, May 8, 1942: Marie J. Regier, Elizabeth Goertz and James Liu sign mission property over to the Chinese.

Missionary conference in China, 1936.
Top Row: (l-r) Martha (Wiens), Philip and August Ewert; Aganetha Fast; W.C. and Matilda (Kliewer) Voth; Henry J. Brown.
2nd Row from top: (l-r) Maria (Miller) Brown; Dr. C.L., Lelia (Roth) and Donald Pannabecker; Sylvia (Tschantz) and S.F. Pannabecker.
3rd Row from top: (l-r) Betty Jean Pannabecker; Leland Voth; Robert Pannabecker; Roland Brown.
Bottom Row: (l-r) David, Ralph and Irene Ewert; Alice Ruth Pannabecker; Anita Pannabecker; Maureen Voth.

Rev. Liu Yueh-Wen, pastor of the Daming Church and 1988 graduate of Yanjing Seminary. He receives no salary from the church but is supported by his farming family. Liu bikes 10 miles to get from his country home to his work at the church. God's grace and the community of faith are the focus of his sermons.

Roland Brown, 1994

Little was known of the fate of the Chinese Christians between 1949 and 1979. Since then remarkable stories of survival have surfaced. By 1989 there were four ordained pastors, 127 voluntary workers, 76 house churches, and 22,681 baptized members in the area once served by General Conference missionaries. Baptismal services were held at Christmas and Easter, and other times as the need arose. The average attendance of churches associated with the former six mission stations was about 18,000. At least one young man from the Puyang church was able to attend seminary. Although the hospital and schools remained in government control, the church thus remained alive.

Myrrl Byler

The Gospel Church in Puyang, founded by Henry J. and Maria (Miller) Brown in about 1919, still stands.

Congo
(known between 1971 and 1996 as Zaire)

Africa Inter-Mennonite Mission (AIMM), formerly called Congo Inland Mission (CIM), was founded in 1912 when the Central Conference of Mennonites and the Defenseless Mennonite Church in Illinois joined their scant resources to begin a work of faith in Congo. Over the years, the belief that more could be accomplished collectively rather than independently has led to a vibrant common witness among Mennonite groups.

Several General Conference people served independently under CIM before the General Conference mission board officially became one of its supporting agencies in 1943. Since then, all COM workers assigned to Africa have been channeled

(Third from left) Kamba, a Baluba, was sent to the Bampende people as one of the pioneer native missionaries. He studied their language and culture. These young men, two of whom are ordained deacons, and the other teachers trace their conversion to Kamba's faithful ministry.

Erwin Rempel, 1991

Ngongo David, outstanding church leader, was one of the first to be invited to sit in on a missionary conference in 1955, in Congo.

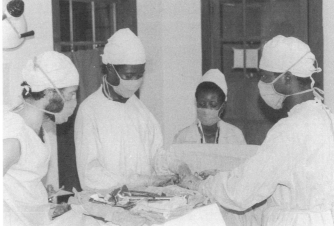

Dr. Dennis Ries and his assistants in surgery at Kalonda Hospital, Congo.

11

"A Congolese Christian man heard a knock at the door in the middle of the night. Someone had come for help and needed money. The only savings he and his wife had was designated for their children's Christmas presents. Out of compassion the man gave that money to the one who needed it. When he told his wife what he had done, she said, 'Thank God we had not spent the money yet. The children will just have to wait till next year for their Christmas presents.'"

—*Delbert Dick*

Women in Charlesville, Congo, extend a warm welcome to an AIMM women's delegation from Canada and the United States in 1971.

Kibundji Kizembe, director of the Bible Institute at Kalonda, Congo.

Congo Mennonite Church leaders in 1987: (l–r) Kabasele, vice president; Tshibelenu, president; Kabaya, treasurer, and Earl Roth, AIMM executive secretary.

A teacher and his students in Congo, 1971.

through this organization. In 1972 CIM became Africa Inter-Mennonite Mission, and began work in several other countries as well.

Much has happened since 1912. In the years leading up to Congo's independence from Belgium in 1960, missionaries established hospitals and schools, taught agricultural development, and preached the gospel. They, along with the Congolese church, experienced the turmoil and violence of the early 1960s. Then, in 1964, the Mennonite church

of Congo received its legal charter from the government and, since 1971, the church programs have been officially run by the Congolese. Although the last AIMM missionaries to Congo completed service in 1998, the mission continues to contribute to the

Erwin Rempel, 1987

CEM (Evangelical Mennonite Church of Congo) gathering near Mbuji Mayi, Congo.

Angela (Albrecht) Rempel

Sikasa, director of Congo's Lycee Miodo, with a sixth-year student.

13

Pastoral ordination: (l-r) Rev. Mukanza Ilunga, Rev. Maratinde Kayenda, and Rev. Kobono Bukasa ordaining Tshiaba Muanza at Mutena, Congo, in 1978.

church's annual budget and participates in special projects.

Today, the AIMM-related Congolese Mennonite churches continue to be among the fastest growing in the Mennonite world community. In 1997, the Congo Mennonite Church (CMCo) had a membership of 83,575 in 900 congregations which were served by 197 ordained persons. The Evangelical Mennonite Church of Congo (CEM)—an offshoot of the CMCo in the 1960s—had more than 21,000 members in 196 congregations.

Mission and church cooperation came to fruition in the mid-1990s with the Rwandan refugee crisis. The Mennonite churches of Congo, Mennonite Central Committee, AIMM, and MBMS International (Mennonite Brethren) sent food, blankets, money, and personnel to refugees in Bukavu, in the Great Lakes area in the east. The refugees, impressed with the witness of these Mennonites and their concern for justice, peace, and reconciliation, asked the Congolese Mennonites to begin a church with them. The first Congolese missionaries arrived in 1998.

Paraguay

German-speaking Mennonite immigrants settled in the Chaco region, as well as the eastern plains of Paraguay, in the late 1920s. Surrounded by native peoples, the Mennonites reached out to them and, later, the Spanish-speaking population. At first COM assisted financially and with personnel, but supervision of the work was done by the German Mennonite Missions Committee.

The Commission on Overseas Mission and Mennonite Board of Missions maintain fraternal relationships with the German-speaking Mennonites, but work primarily with the Spanish-speaking Mennonite churches developing throughout the country. A key ministry of both groups is the Evangelical Mennonite Center of Theology of Asuncion (CEMTA). The institute provides a strong program of four-year studies in theology and sacred music, with classes taught in Spanish and German.

Kornelius Isaac, a Paraguayan missionary under the German Mennonite Mission Board, was killed by the Moro Indians in Paraguay on an exploratory visit in 1958.

Mary Isaac, widow of Kornelius, and her family shortly after the death of her husband at the hands of the Moro Indians in Paraguay.

Jeannie (Hughes) Zehr, 1985

CEMTA, located in Asuncion, Paraguay, provides opportunities for Latin Americans to further their studies in theology and music.

Mark J. Epp

Allan Friesen, COM worker, visits with a CEMTA student after class.

15

ACCEPTED BY GOD

Bent with age and in pain, Pataitine Bai crawled up the church steps in Champa. No matter how miserable she felt, Pataitine attended services regularly. She was not one to give up. Children teased her when they met her on the road, saying, "There is no place for you in heaven, Pataitine Bai," to which she replied, "I know the Lord has a place ready for me."

In her younger years, Pataitine's husband was afraid that other men might look at her. One day, in a fit of jealous rage, he tried to cut off her nose, leaving an ugly scar as evidence that he almost succeeded. She fled for help and protection to the home of P.A. and Elizabeth (Dickman) Penner, the first General Conference Mennonite missionaries to India. They took her to Bilaspur to have her nose stitched down. Her husband was imprisoned and later died.

One of the first converts to Christianity in our mission, Palaitine worked in the Penner's home for many years. She and her second husband Chandu accepted Christ and were baptized in 1910. Throughout the years their children were employed in mission hospitals and schools. One of their grandchildren participated in the Mennonite Central Committee Visitors Abroad program.

Having lived a saintly life, Palaitine was publicly honored in 1960, at the 60th anniversary celebration of the India mission.

—*Benjamin Sawatzky and Kathryn (Loutham) Jantzen*

Pataitine Bai, early convert in India in the GC mission.

Benjamin Sawatzky

GOPAL'S EIGHTEEN-YEAR PRAYER

The year was about 1915, in India. Ezra and Elizabeth (Geiger) Steiner, on an evangelistic tour for several weeks, had one more village to visit before going home. The community buzzed with excitement as hundreds of people sold their wares at the local market. Suddenly, everyone's attention was focused on these white foreigners who were singing and telling stories of the Savior.

Gopal Das and two other weavers heard the music, and pressed closer. Deeply moved, Gopal said to his friends, "Surely these people are of God. They will hear our plea." When the singing stopped, the weavers begged the Steiners to come to their own village and teach them about God. Weary and committed to going home the next day, the Steiners declined. That evening the weavers again implored them to come, but were refused.

The weavers would not give up. The next morning as the Steiners prepared to leave, the men approached them again. Impressed by their sincerity, the Steiners prayed and decided that Ezra would accompany them and Elizabeth would go home.

Late that afternoon, excited villagers welcomed Gopal, his fellow weavers, and the first white missionary they had ever seen. Word spread quickly. Friends and relatives of Gopal heard the Christian message that evening and declared their intention to follow the "Jesus way."

Gopal, already a Christian, had waited for someone to come and evangelize his people for 18 years. Meanwhile, he had done what he could, telling other weavers about Jesus. Two years before Ezra Steiner went to India, Gopal had walked 80 miles in one direction to ask a group of Christians for help, but was refused. Then he walked 110 miles south to another group, only to be turned down again. Finally, on that day in the market, God had heard his plea.

Gopal made a difference. Because of him, others came to know Christ. Twenty men and women were baptized in Gopal's village in 1917. Two years later, through the work of Peter J. and Agnes (Harder) Wiens, 108 were baptized. In 1921 there was a mass baptism of 96 adults pledging their faith to Jesus Christ.

—*S.T. Moyer*

Missionaries Ezra and Elizabeth (Geiger) Steiner, who responded to Gopal's plea.

Gopal Das, the weaver.

17

HAVE HANDICAP, WILL TRAVEL

Missionary Frank Enns in Congo was moved to compassion when he met Nshidi Lazarre, an intelligent orphan boy whose family had rejected him because of his physical difficulties. Enns brought

Pastor Nshidi Lazarre was able to visit distant places with the help of these boys.

Tina Quiring

Nshidi to Nyanga station and enrolled him in the boarding school.

In 1928 doctors from Luebo, the neighboring Presbyterian Mission, treated the sick at Nyanga. Seeing this bright-eyed boy, they too were moved to compassion and took Nshidi back to Luebo for medical treatment, where he stayed for about 30 years.

By 1939 Nshidi had completed four years of Bible school in Mutoto. He became the chaplain in the hospital and later in the school at Bulape. In time the Presbyterian church appointed him as an evangelist to a village in Banzela Luebo. At age 37, he married Biabo Kamba, a young Christian woman. As newlyweds they gave leadership for seven years to the recently organized Bible school in Mutena.

Upon his request, Nshidi was granted a leave of absence and returned to his home area at Nyanga, where a royal welcome greeted him. People gladly listened as he shared his testimony and preached the gospel in Mennonite churches. The mission leaders asked the Presbyterians to release Nshidi for service in the Mennonite Church, his original faith family. During the turbulence of independence in 1960s and accompanying the tribal wars, Rev. Nshidi and his family returned to Nyanga, where he was the teacher and treasurer for the Bible school.

It became difficult for Nshidi to walk long distances and impossible for him to ride a bike. A cart made of discarded motorcycle wheels and powered by Bible school students allowed him to travel as far as 50 miles to carry on his ministries. Many people decided to follow Jesus through Nshidi's faithful work.

—*Tina Quiring*

ALL IDOLS HAVE TO GO

Henry and Maria (Miller) Brown attended a wedding in Huang Ping, China, around 1914. Mr. Liu, who took an active part in the festivities, invited the Browns to visit his home in a nearby village after the celebration ended.

Arriving in Mr. Liu's home, the Browns were served tea. Mr. Liu then took Mrs. Brown into the rear of the yard to meet his wife, and returned to fetch Mr. Brown.

In order to get to the backyard, they had to walk through the kitchen. Mr. Liu stopped, pointed to a "kettle god" pasted on the wall and said emphatically, "It is enough! Tear him down. He has made me suffer enough. For years I have been tormented by the evil ones. Now I believe in Jesus. He has set me free and healed me. All idols have to go, for I will worship only the Savior. These powers of darkness have to go."

While Mr. Brown removed the kitchen god, Mr. Liu ran into the next room to collect the god of riches. Both were forced into the stove and, as they watched the flames devour them, Mr. Liu said, "Now they are gone. Let the missionary lead us in a word of prayer to the true God." At the close of the prayer, the Christians in the room said a loud "Amen."

—*Henry J. Brown,* Chips of Experience

Missionary Tidbits from India

- Two years of India's Hindi language study doesn't lead to perfect proficiency. A worker from another mission was the guest of Vernelle (Schroeder) Waltner and her husband, Orlando. In the evening Vernelle instructed the cook what he was to do for breakfast the next morning. She showed him the "tea cozy" (a cover for the teapot) and asked him to put it on the "tea." The cook nodded his head as though he understood her instructions. The next morning he proudly walked into the dining room wearing the tea cozy on his head! Only the Waltners and their guest knew where it really belonged! —Told by Orlando and Vernelle Waltner and children on a visit to a village in India.

- Martha Burkhalter was surely one of the most colorful characters who served in India under the GC mission board. At one of the first mission conferences, Ken Bauman got up and made an impassioned plea for something—probably no one knows any more what it was that he wanted. Martha B. did not understand either, but she was so sure of Ken, that she got up to suggest: "I don't know what Ken wants, but let's let him have it." Now that's loyalty!

- Agramuti, the *ayah* (helper) for the family of Drs. Ella (Garber) and Harvey Bauman in India, had a son, Freddie. He and the doctors' son Kenneth Bauman were good friends. One day Kenneth disappeared. When his parents found out that he had gone off to eat with the ayah's family, they were upset. They were concerned that Kenneth was taking food from them. Dr. Ella asked him what kind of curry they had. Kenneth very evasively said "meat," which was very expensive and hard to get. His mother chided him, so he explained, "Oh, that's OK. They didn't have to pay for it; it was rat curry!"

Apostle to Women

Bundi Bai, born to a wealthy family near Bhopal, India, was orphaned in the Great Famine of 1898-1900. She was only eight years old. Like thousands of other children, Bundi was placed in a mission orphanage. Her new home was the Mukti Mission in Pune, founded by Pandita Ramabai, one of the pioneers of women's rights in India.

Mathilde (Ensz) Penner and her faithful Bible women. Standing: (l-r) Bundi Bai, Penner, and Munika Bai. Sitting: Bimola Bai and Rupa Bai.

W.F. Unruh Album, MLA

20

At age 12, Bundi became gravely ill. All despaired of her life except Pandita Ramabai. She felt God had a great ministry for Bundi and prayed fervently for her recovery. When Bundi regained her health, she set her heart on working among the women of Bombay.

Bundi's plans changed when John Walters, headmaster of the Methodist Middle School for Boys in Raipur, married her in 1904. They lived in Raipur where John taught school and Bundi served as housemother in the boys' dormitory. Her dream of working with women, however, never left her.

After many years of ministry with the Methodists, John and Bundi joined the General Conference Mennonite mission. John pastored the Janjgir church, taught in the Bible school, served as conference treasurer, edited the conference periodical *Mennonite Bandu*, and later pastored the Jagdeeshpur church.

Bundi, meanwhile, was able to fulfill her dream of ministering to women. The loss of several children had driven her to find comfort in God's Word, and over the years she had become very well versed in it—even though she had only a fourth-grade education. With the Mennonites, she joined the ranks of the "Bible women" who were trained and paid to teach the Bible. An assertive woman, Bundi demanded modesty in dress, boldness, and discipline of those who worked with her. But there was no limit to her compassion and kindness. Her loving heart and generous hands reached out to the needy, especially to widows and orphans.

—*Helen Kornelsen*

KEEPING THE LANTERN LIT

Many villagers came to Sh'a Pulu, the "old pastor" in Nyanga, Congo, for Christian counseling. In his wise, humorous ways he would guide them. Years after his wife died, he married Mama Lusamba, a widow from another village called Kananga. Mama Lusamba soon made friends and was loved because of her sunny, outgoing personality. Her husband once said to missionary Eudene Keidel, "Since Mama Lusamba came here, we have church every day. She visits the sick and dying, and helps the poor in the village."

Mama Lusamba cared for Sh'a Pulu when his health failed. She often asked missionary Grace Harder for a little kerosene to keep a lantern burning through the night, allowing her to be available to Sh'a Pulu. During the day she took short naps on a bamboo mat and lay on the floor near him, in case he should call.

As the months went by, Sh'a Pulu became weaker. Mama Lusamba was his constant companion until he died. A week after his burial, the missionaries participated in a large outdoor meeting at Mama Lusamba's home. It was a service of praise, remembering a man who impacted many lives. It was also a farewell service for Mama Lusamba, who would return to her home village, in keeping with African custom.

In gratitude for what Mama Lusamba meant to the church at Nyanga, the people gathered enough money to fly her by MAF (Mission Aviation Fellowship) plane back to Kananga, where she lived among her own people.

—*Grace (Hiebner) Harder and Eudene (King) Keidel*

Kuamba Charles, of the Lulua tribe, was a long time pastor of a congregation in the area of Tshikapa, Congo. During the Baluba-Lulua tribal conflict, he was approached one day by his fellow tribesmen. "To which tribe do you lend your support?" they wanted to know. "To neither," Kuamba Charles replied. "When I became a believer, I became a member of a new tribe, the tribe of the Lord Jesus."

Gordon Claassen

Young men reading "Who Are the Mennonites?" by Levi Keidel, Congo.

21

A MAN OF INTEGRITY

In 1930 James C. Liu and Stephen Wang came to study at Bluffton and Bethel Colleges in North America. Both graduated in 1932 and returned to the General Conference Mennonite Mission in Kaizhou (Puyang), where James served as principal at Hua Mei High School until 1946.

That year, following the Yellow River flood, James and his wife Hazel joined Mennonite Central Committee. Hazel, a nurse, was in charge of a country clinic while James served as an interpreter and sometimes worked on translations in the office.

Hard times followed as China became Communist, and as the Cultural Revolution spread throughout China in 1966. One day the Red Guards took all of the Lius' possessions, and declared that since some of their belongings came from the United States, James was an enemy of China. On September 18, 1968, the principal called James into the school to take part in the Cultural Revolution movement. He was seized and locked up, and endured three years of imprisonment in his own schoolroom. He was severely criticized for being an intellectual and a Christian. He was not allowed to see Hazel. He was ridiculed and humiliated by students, and accused of being an American spy and a running dog.

He had to clean toilets and plant vegetables. If the work was not satisfactory, he was severely scolded and tortured. Finally in July 1971 James Liu was released because the authorities could not find fault with him. He was able to go home.

Nothing was heard from James Liu for many years, but missionary friends always remembered him in prayer. Marie J. (Regier) (Frantz) Janzen wrote a letter to James but it was returned, marked "Refused." She recognized his handwriting and knew that he was alive. Eventually, however, contact resumed. On August 10, 1973, James wrote to Marie: "There is not a church in Hengyang, nor a house church. The only church we have here is heart-church…"

In 1985 James Liu was able to visit Puyang (formerly Kaizhou) again. The magistrate of the city greeted him and told him, "Your mission and school made great contributions to the Puyang people. If you go to America again, be sure to tell this to the missionaries and their children. They can come any time and stay here as long as they wish. They are welcome in Puyang."

—*from* Christians True in China, *edited by Robert Kreider*

Hazel and James Liu, 1987.

Robert Kreider

John Sommer

Extended family of James and Hazel Liu in 1988 in China.

GIFT OF MERCY

An angry mob in Belladula, India, threatened to kill the staunch, young convert Kriparam Ghore, and all who had come from Champa for his baptism on March 25, 1926. "Perhaps we should postpone Kripa's baptism," the evangelist suggested. "It is not safe. The family has already locked up his wife, Phulquar, so that she cannot be baptized with him."

Erect and fearless, Kriparam faced the tense crowd. Only a timely intervention by his father prevented another beating by his uncle. The father said, "Brother, we have given life to Kriparam, but we have failed to give him the kind of teaching and example that his new religion has given him. What has happened, has happened. Let it be."

Kripa, conscious of the deep hurt he caused his family, turned sadly away from them. To his waiting Christian friends he said, "Do not be afraid to baptize me. The Lord Jesus has appeared to me in a vision and has given me peace. If anyone wants to kill me for the sake of the Lord Jesus, I am ready to die. He is my Lord. Him only will I serve."

The evangelist, moved by the thoughtful silence around him, said, "Kripa has a firm faith. He has requested that we baptize him today. This is the day that the Lord has made. I am prepared to die with him, if that is necessary."

Kriparam was baptized and rechristened Kripadan, "the Gift of Mercy," and accepted as a member of the Bharatiya General Conference Mennonite Church. Immediately after his baptism,

Kripadan Ghore, Indian pastor, and his family.

Helen Kornelsen

Kripadan was banished from his home. His wife was able to join him early the next morning. On April 17 she, too, followed Christ in baptism.

The same courage and firmness of purpose characterized Kripadan's long life and rich ministry in the Bharatiya General Conference Mennonite Church. Through the years he brought many people to Christ, including his own relatives. At his retirement in 1966, Kripadan mused, "Every opportunity to preach the gospel is a joy to me."

—*Helen Kornelsen*

KEEPER OF THE KEYS

Pastor Kazadi Matthieu was at the center of the unfolding story of two Mennonite churches in Congo. Born in the South Kasai region in the early 1900s to a Muluba sub-chief and his eighth wife, Kazadi was baptized as an infant. Later he found employment in Djoko Punda, at a new mission station planted by Congo Inland Mission.

Upon graduation from the Djoka Punda Bible School, Kazadi served his Lord and his church. He was the first Congolese leader to build a major regional church center on his own, the first president of the Congo Mennonite Church (CMZ), and the first Congolese Mennonite to tour North America as a fraternal delegate of his church. A familiar figure on the platform at church conferences and in business sessions, Kazadi's inspirational preaching and alert, probing questions became his trademark.

In 1960, the year Congo became independent from Belgium, the air was filled with tension. Everything was in turmoil. Army officers urged missionaries to leave, while some of the African pastors felt the missionaries should stay and suffer with them. After much soul-searching, Kazadi encouraged the missionaries to leave, believing that the Lord would bring them back. They heeded his advice, and turned over to him the keys to their homes.

Shortly after, while Kazadi was staying at a missionary's house, he bravely faced 30 Bakuba warriors armed with spears and broad-bladed machetes, ready for action.

"Life to you!" he called to them. "What is your problem?"

They had come to forcefully remove Kazadi and his family, ordering him to go back to his own people, the Baluba. As he faced these warriors who had been his friends, he heard a commotion behind him. Kazadi's own tribesmen suddenly emerged from behind the house, ready to fight. He rose quickly and called out, "There is no reason to fight. Call your chiefs; bring them here; we will talk and settle the matter."

The crowd dispersed. Kazadi sat there, pondering the future. Forty years of work was crumbling, and he could do nothing about it. He had to leave.

Forced to flee tribal conflict in the early 1960s, Kazadi found thousands of refugees in the South Kasai, where he immediately organized fellow Mennonites into clusters for prayer, worship, and mutual aid. Cut off by distance and political conflict from the mother church, Kazadi eventually became the president of a second church conference, the Evangelical Mennonite Community. In his later years he lived in Kinshasa, where he spoke in area churches until his strength waned.

—*James Bertsche and Levi Keidel*

Kazadi Matthieu, Congo Mennonite church leader in 1980.

James Juhnke

GOD NEUTRALIZES THE POISON

One mid-afternoon in the early 1950s, I visited the village of Kokoikombe, Congo. Our teacher Difuanda was not feeling well. When I asked him to explain, this is what he told me:

These village people are rebellious. They don't want the gospel. They are afraid it will ruin their traditions. For the most part, they ignore me. They let me do what I wish with a small group of children every morning.

One day an old village man squatted outside my hut to talk. He wanted to know why they had been unable to kill me like they had killed other outsiders. I asked him what he meant.

His reply: "Do you remember when you asked our children to bring you some coins to give as a birthday present for your Jesus? Before we gave them to our children, we rubbed poison on them that was to kill you. It didn't work. Later, when you sent children with water-gourds to bring you drinking water from the spring, we dropped poison powder into the gourds when the children were returning. You used the water, and nothing happened. Then, when a village hunter killed an antelope, we sent you a piece of poisoned hip meat as a gift. You and your family ate it, and nothing happened. So we are wondering why you don't die, like other people."

I told him that Jesus was protecting me, because he wanted them to listen to what I was trying to teach them. But none of this won their favor. One day village men came and beat up on me, my wife, and children. I saw three men trampling on the back of my 14-year-old son; I don't know how he escaped alive. My body is still sore from the beating. That's why I'm not feeling well.

—*Levi Keidel*

CONGOLESE MISSIONARIES LAUNCH OUT

A long-held dream of Congolese Mennonites came true in 1998 when they were able to send forth Philemon and Kingambo Begela as their first missionaries. Their destination: Bukavu, in the eastern Great Lakes region of Congo. Their ministry came on the heels of the civil war and a refugee crisis that followed a campaign of genocide in neighboring Rwanda. A nucleus of believers had already formed in Bukavu as a result of Mennonite relief work.

The Begelas hold masters degrees from the Bangui Theological Seminary in Central African Republic. Philemon had a vision of leading the Congo Mennonite Church in a pioneer foreign missions outreach in sub-Saharan Africa. Though there was chaos in Congo, and inflation raged at 400 percent, he had discovered the biblical truth that "We look not to the things that are seen but to the things that are unseen... the things that are unseen are eternal" (2 Cor. 4:18).

Their move to Bukavu was held up for 18 months while civil strife continued in the country. As the new believers in Bukavu awaited the Begelas' arrival, they gathered to worship and encourage each other. After the Begelas arrived in 1998, they baptized ten members into the newly formed Mennonite church.

—*Tina Block Ediger*

Refugee camp in eastern Congo.

Philemon Begela with his wife Kingambo Pauline and child, missionaries to Bukavu, Congo.

Richard Steiner

KEEPING FAITH IN THE FAMILY

Ratni was among hundreds of graduates of the Annie Funk Memorial School, well known in Janjgir, India. Christian teachers introduced her to the Bible and Jesus, whom she accepted into her life.

After completing school, however, Ratni returned home to discover her parents had arranged for her to marry a Hindu boy from a distant village. Ratni was not pleased, but there was little she could do.

The wedding took place despite her feelings, and Ratni went with her husband to a new people and a new home. She took her Bible, which she read often as she prayed for guidance.

Twenty years later, a stranger visited missionaries Curt and Olga (Schultz) Claassen in Champa. It was Ratni's husband who had come to arrange for the baptism of their 18-year-old son. Through the years, Ratni's faithful witness had borne fruit. In time her husband and many others from that village were also baptized.

—Mary (Schrag) Pauls

Ratni, fourth from left, with her family. Also in the picture are missionaries Jake and Dorothy (Andres) Giesbrecht, and a visiting relative from Canada.

Hilda (Giesbrecht) Reed

27

Missionary Levi Keidel and Pastor Mayamba with a poor widow giving her corn offering to God.

A MAN OF PRAYER

With a limited education and a few years of Bible school, Congolese pastor Mayamba was ordained to the ministry and served faithfully for many years. His parish was a heavily-populated palm-oil plantation owned by the Lever Brothers. From 1951 to 1960, I regularly visited the area, and we became close friends.

I remember those nights when I slept on a mosquito net-covered cot in Mayamba's living room, and was awakened in the early mornings by Mayamba's voice raised in bedside prayers with his wife.

With the coming of Congo's political independence in 1960, wars drove Mayamba and his large family back to their distant tribal homeland. Mayamba sold bicycles to make a living. One day, six of his fellow tribesmen from the capital city of Kinshasa, 800 miles distant, called him to be their spiritual shepherd. Mayamba accepted their invitation, and in due time his congregation grew to over 1,200 members.

On his deathbed Mayamba said, "Everything I learned about the pastoral ministry, I learned from Levi." I gratefully accepted the family's invitation, 500 miles away, to conduct daily evening devotions in their front yard the week following the funeral.

—*Levi Keidel*

HOLDING FAST THROUGH CHINA'S REVOLUTION

Stephen Wang was born November 13, 1905. His mother was a peasant with bound feet; his father, a lowly scholar. Converted to Christianity, Stephen's parents became evangelists for the General Conference Mennonite Mission in China's Henan province. In 1927, while on a preaching tour, both his parents were shot by wandering bandits. Only his mother survived.

Stephen and his classmate James Liu attended Bluffton and Bethel colleges in the United States for two years, graduating from the latter in 1932. Upon his return to China, Stephen served as academic dean and teacher in the Hua Mei High School in Kaizhou (Puyang). His wife Margaret Zhang became the school's only female teacher. They fled Puyang in 1937, when the Japanese invaded the area. In 1950, Stephen and Margaret moved to Changchun, where he was a respected faculty member at Northeastern Normal University. Margaret headed up a residential district of 300 university families.

The tumult of China's frequent political movements affected Stephen. In 1957, he was demoted and publicly humiliated. His daughter and son-in-law were severely injured by machine-gun fire during the Cultural Revolution.

In 1969 Stephen and Margaret were sent to the countryside for four years of "reeducation" under the Cultural Revolution. Stephen watched the pigs and chickens so they would not spoil the crops, and sometimes collected manure. He kept his dignity and gained respect among the people, many of whom became his friends.

Stephen's children wondered how he, the son of an impoverished family, was able to become a university professor. He said, "I could not have gone to school for even one year without the help of the church. I give credit for my education—from primary school, to the university, to going abroad—wholly to Mennonite missions, both in China and the United States.

Stephen, who credits his long life to optimism, radiates inner peace and joy. Known as the "Christian professor," he holds no bitterness nor regret, an attitude his colleagues find difficult to understand.

Stephen's faith never wavered. From 1950 to 1957, with Margaret and her mother, he attended the one church allowed to remain open in Changchun. In 1979 when churches reopened, he attended services until old age and deafness prevented it. His spirit is completely rooted in Christianity. He grew up with it; it is in his blood.

Stephen and Margaret's children respect their parents' Christian faith but do not practice it. Still they live in hope that one day they will.

—*From* Christians True in China,
edited by Robert Kreider

Margaret and Stephen Wang of China, 1981.

![Lengua Indian Isaac Epp with briefcase, leaving on a Sunday mission.](photo)

Eleanor Mathies

Lengua Indian Isaac Epp with briefcase, leaving on a Sunday mission.

THE WORD COMES HOME AMONG THE LENGUA

In the late 1920s, Mennonites from Manitoba settled in the Menno Colony of the Paraguayan Chaco on land that belonged to the friendly, nomadic Lengua people. The Lengua, given employment by the Mennonites, soon learned Low German. Some even gave themselves "Mennonite" names.

A few years later Mennonite immigrants from Russia who had settled in the Fernheim Colony began mission work among the Lengua and Nivacle (formerly Chulupi) groups. After seven years of outreach, the first seven converts were baptized.

One of the converts was Isaac Epp, a Lengua. A quiet, wise man, Isaac learned to read and write, and studied the Scriptures as they were made available in his Lengua mother tongue. He became the spiritual leader of his people. During the week Isaac and his wife worked for the Mennonite settlers, but on weekends they returned to the little village which had been established for the Lenguas of the area.

Isaac led prayer meetings on Fridays and Saturdays, and early, lengthy church services on Sunday mornings. Everyone respected Isaac, whose father had been a tribal family group leader. After evening services, small groups gathered around a fire wherever someone was able to read a portion of Scripture. The fellowship continued until quite late.

—*Eleanor Mathies*

FINDING A FAITH THAT WORKS

Jai Singh Bagh's initiation into the spirit world of the Hindu priesthood failed. Try as he may, nothing worked. Disillusioned and disappointed, Jai Singh disregarded the injunctions of his elders to have nothing to do with the Christians in his village. Instead, he sought them out. Secretly, Jai Singh began to read the Bible.

The following summer, cholera struck the village of Kutela, India, in the Saraipali area. Many villagers died, including Jai Singh's aunt. He, too, was struck with the illness. This experience so soon after his initiation raised further doubts in his mind. Where, now, were the magic powers to ward off the evils of cholera? Where were the powers to heal him? These questions tormented Jai Singh. To his surprise, he discovered that his father also had doubts. Together, they prayed to the Christian God for Jai Singh's full recovery. God heard their prayers. Jai Singh recovered.

When he was 22, Jai Singh married Kamala. Though the marriage was arranged by his parents, Jai Singh and Kamala learned to love each other, and their happiness increased when children were added to the family. By this time, Jai Singh had nearly forgotten his cholera experience and near-death fears.

About that time, Din Bandhu, a Christian *sadhu* (preacher), came and proclaimed that he had powers to heal the sick. Many heard him preach, including Jai Singh, Kamala, and their mothers. Jai Singh could not forget the message; he was determined to find out more.

The next stop for the sadhu was Cana, a village only six miles from Kutela. Jai Singh and Kamala, with their two little children, walked to Kutela to hear the sadhu. Impressed with his message, they stayed for the evening meeting. Jai Singh was convinced that what the sadhu preached, he desired and needed. Lost in deep thought, he almost missed the sadhu's closing remarks: "Tomorrow we will have a baptismal service in the church in Girola. All those who want to follow the Lord Jesus Christ may come and be baptized."

Reflecting on the day's events, Jai Singh and Kamala agreed that they wanted to be baptized. When they returned to their home that evening, they found everyone still awake. Until late into the night, Jai Singh related everything he and Kamala had heard and seen. In conclusion he said, "Tomorrow I am going to be baptized. I want to be a Christian."

News spread throughout the village, and the people murmured their disapprovals. Yet Jai Singh and Kamala were not deterred. They returned to Girola the next morning and told the sadhu that they wanted to be baptized. The sadhu and the pastors asked them several questions, and the couples' answers satisfied them. Happily, they knelt with others and were baptized.

When Jai Singh opened his eyes after the prayer, his startled gaze fell upon his father kneeling beside him. He, too, was being baptized. Some time later his mother also confessed Christ through baptism.

—*Helen Kornelsen*

Pastor Jai Singh Bagh as a young man.

Anil Bagh, his son, is grateful that his father became a Christian. Christianity has given his family a chance at a good education and the desire to serve the Lord. All the children of Jai Singh Bagh and his wife are in Christian service.

31

Serving God in the Kitchen

In the 1930s life was simple at the General Conference Mennonite mission station in Puyang, China. Or was it complicated? Missionaries did not have the use of electricity, running water, telephones, or cars. But hired help in the home eased such handicaps considerably.

Sylvia (Tschantz) Pannabecker liked to cook but, since the family had a cook, she seldom got a chance. One day Sylvia decided to bake a cake. It was a complicated procedure because the oven was heated with patties of charcoal dust. She started to mix the ingredients when a woman from a nearby village came to call. When the visitor left, Sylvia began again to work on the cake, but was called away in a few minutes to talk with another visitor.

When this happened the third time, Shing Jing jia, the cook, turned to Sylvia and said, "I'll finish the cake. You serve God in the front room and I'll serve God in the kitchen." Sylvia, delighted with the cook's sense of call, told the story often.

—*Alice Ruth (Pannabecker) Ramseyer*

A Mennonite Directs Elite Prison

Congo's central government ordered Mbuyamba André, a quiet, intense, unassuming Mennonite, to direct the prison at Gbadolite where President Mobutu sent political prisoners to be executed.

A 1976 graduate of Kinshasa's Superior Institute, André pastored, studied, and served as a prison chaplain before he was summoned to Gbadolite. There, André found the prisoners' morale deplorable. Afraid, sullen, and angry, they were without hope. André was ordered never to come into the prisoners' presence without the guards' protection.

A most difficult task for André was to inform the prisoners of their execution dates. He determined that the gospel of Christ must make a difference in this dark and hopeless situation.

André's request to begin chapel services, however, was repeatedly denied; the government feared that such liberty might foment revolt. He put his directorship on the line, took full responsibility for his actions, and began chapel services. Prisoners responded enthusiastically, and many found new hope and life in Christ.

Finally the prisoners received André as their friend, and he was able to walk among them without the guards' protection. The presence of Christ changed the atmosphere in the prison. A shaft of light and the love of God had pierced the cloud of darkness and despair.

—*Peter Buller*

We Danced When the Moon Was High

The breathing of water buffalo tied to a post near my cot kept me awake in a farmer's yard that hot April night in 1961. Missionary Helen Kornelsen was introducing me, a new arrival, to a mission church celebration in Ambikapur, India. We had arrived late afternoon and were welcomed by Lily and Puran Banwar, the Indian missionaries stationed there. As was their tradition with guests, the women of the church washed our feet. We enjoyed a love feast late in the evening. Then we returned to the farmer's place for a few hours of sleep. When the moon had risen, we would return to the church to continue the celebration.

Helen and I went to bed with our clothes on because there was no privacy. Since I had never slept outdoors, I lay awake on my cot, skeptical, contemplating the nearness of the water buffalo. When the moon was high, in the distance we heard the beating of drums. "It's time to go," whispered Helen, and off we went, accompanied by the other women who shared the yard with us.

That moonlit night, I danced for the first time in my life! These new Christians sang and danced to the stories of the Old Testament, which had become part of their oral history.

The joy was rooted deep in the story of how the church was formed in Ambikapur. Missionary Adah (Good Burkhalter) Wenger reported in 1952, "Perhaps no one can tell when, where, and how Christian influence had filtered in, but when we [missionaries] first entered, we found a small group of Christians holding

Pastor Puran Banwar and his wife Lily in Ambikapur, India, 1962.

various positions in Ambikapur, the capital city—even a Christian mother doing private teaching in the palaces for the household of the Maharaja."

These people, the Uraons, were Aboriginal animists who were open to the gospel. The Home Missions Committee of the Bharatiya General Conference Mennonite Church assigned Puran and Lily to work with them.

33

Footwashing in India.

S.F. Pannabecker

When the Banwars first arrived in 1954, they were met with opposition. The attitude of the people soon changed, however, when they saw a tattoo on Lily's arm, which identified her as a member of their extended tribe. Puran and Lily adopted the Uraon way of life, ate their food, and identified with them. Over the years, they won the hearts of the people. Those who had opposed them when they first arrived became their friends.

The efforts of the Banwars resulted in the birth of the Calvary Mennonite Church which, at this night event, was accepted as a member of the Bharatiya General Conference Mennonite Church. During the Banwars' 17 years of ministry to the Uraons, three churches and one school were established. Church membership grew from 10 to 571 adults, with 700 children.

—*Tina Block Ediger*

COMMISSIONED FROM BIRTH

"You shall be called Samuel," whispered Ruth Bai to her newborn son on March 28, 1918. "We shall dedicate you to the Lord." Samuel's deeply committed parents, Balamdas and Ruth Bai Stephen, did their best to raise their children in an atmosphere of love and reverence to God. Samuel knew that he had been dedicated to the Lord.

Both Balamdas and Ruth Bai survived India's terrible famine of 1893-94, with the help of the Methodist Mission. Then they came to work with Agnes and P.J. Wiens in Mauhadih, becoming some of the first Mennonites in India.

Samuel attended elementary and high school in Mauhadih, Raipur, and Dhamtari. In 1936 he returned to Mauhadih to teach in the boys' middle school. The government inspector, impressed with Samuel's teaching abilities, recommended him for a diploma in teaching in Jagalpur. During his absence from Mauhadih in 1937, the floods inundated the village. The boys' school was transferred to Jagdeeshpur, 30 miles to the south, and named the Jansen Memorial Higher Secondary School (JMHSS) in honor of its benefactor in Kansas.

Upon completing his studies at Jagalpur in 1944, Samuel was invited to teach at JMHSS. That same year he married Helen Pennalal, a teacher at Funk Memorial Girls' School in Janjgir. They made their home in Jagdeeshpur, and Helen soon found her place at JMHSS. The next year Samuel became the new headmaster.

The student body increased, the facilities were expanded, and courses changed to meet the educational needs of the day.

In 1956, Samuel and Helen came to the United States for further study. Samuel earned a master of education degree while Helen took classes in home economics. After their return to India, Samuel continued his role as principal of JMHSS until 1979 and, for the next three years, was the manager of Mennonite mission schools in Champa, Janjgir, and Jagdeeshpur.

The church, always dear to Samuel and Helen, involved them in many ways. Samuel was ordained in 1966. On the conference level Samuel has served as secretary, chairman, and treasurer. He feels that his greatest contribution, however, was educating students at JMHSS, where a large number of key pastors, hospital workers, teachers, and principals studied.

—*Helen Kornelsen*

Standing, l–r: Helen Stephen and her daughter Shireen. Sitting, l–r: son Anand, husband Samuel Stephen, and his mother Ruth Bai Stephen.

Munjila Muandu, coordinator of Bandundu Region, Kikwit, Congo.

Erwin Rempel, 1984

LONG HIKE

When Munjila Muandu was named coordinator of women's work for Congo's Bandundu region, she began her job with a trip that has characterized her dedication ever since. She left her family of nine children at home in Kikwit, and visited 12 churches. From February 2 to May 9, 1984, with no vehicle and no resources to pay for transportation, she traveled on foot most of the way, usually with a companion. Many kilometers separated some of the villages.

When Munjila arrived at each church, she greeted the people and called them together for a meeting. She came to learn from them, and to witness to them. She wanted to present Christ in such a way that those who had not yet accepted him would do so. During Munjila's visit to these churches, she reported a total attendance of over 4,000, with 445 decisions for Christ.

Although Munjila did not attend a Bible training school, she took Theological Education by Extension (TEE) courses for five years.

Muandu, Munjila's husband, is a lay leader in the church and a merchant by trade. He has encouraged his wife in this ministry, caring for their family in her absence. In addition to ministry, Munjila keeps the family fed by working in their fields of peanuts, manioc, and corn.

—*Angela (Albrecht) Rempel*

Miracles in Jagdeeshpur

"I am amazed that God wants to use me," said Amritius (Amrit) Sonwani when he was installed as a nursing superintendent. He was the first Indian to hold this position at the Sewa Bhawan Hospital in Jagdeeshpur, India, in the hospital's 37-year history. Amrit had many talents. He beautified the hospital grounds for the patients to enjoy. He initiated a rural health program by training local health teachers. He organized an 11-day eye camp for cataract removal, attended by 500 patients from 124 villages. He gave time and energy to family planning programs, which were encouraged by the government.

The spiritual aspects of nursing care were highest priority for Amrit, who would work closely with the Bible woman Pushpalata John and Chaplain Abrahim Nand. Joseph J. Duerksen, a missionary doctor, remembers an exploratory surgery he performed on a critically ill woman. Unable to do anything definitive for her, Dr. Duerksen closed the patient and took her to the recovery room. Amrit, seeing the woman breathing her last with gasps of agony, called Dr. Duerksen for help. They put medications into her IV, but Dr. Duerksen knew that they would never reach the patient in time to take any effect. Before their eyes, however, the patient suddenly improved, proceeded to recover, and went home well. Dr. Duerksen knew that Amrit was praying silently, and he knew he had witnessed a miracle.

Missionaries held Amrit in high esteem. His keen sense of humor often helped him and the staff over rough spots. He knew how to deal with his people, whether it was informing them of their responsibilities to pay for services rendered, or to reprimand a relative of a patient for using old instead of fresh dung to wash the floor of the ward!

One day Amrit interpreted for a visiting professor from the Mennonite Biblical Seminary. When the speaker expressed a thought in idiomatic English, to the delight of the missionaries present, Amrit matched it with an idiomatic Hindi phrase that perfectly conveyed the thought. None of the missionaries would have been able to accomplish this!

In 1990 Amrit and his wife Kamala attended the Mennonite World Conference in Winnipeg, Manitoba. At the Sunday morning communion service, a hippie sat down beside Amrit, which angered him. How dare such a person darken this beautiful event! Gradually he recognized this stranger as a follower of Christ. For Amrit, it was a "conversion experience" when he was able to accept the young man as a brother in Christ.

— *Joseph J. Duerksen, Homer Janzen, Larry Kehler, and Helen Kornelsen*

Amritius Sonwani, nursing superintendent at Sewa Bhawan Hospital, Jagdeeshpur, India, 1971.

Verney Unruh

A DETERMINED VOICE

Baba Kafutshi was one of the first two girls who attended the teachers' training institute in Mukedi,

Kakesa Samuel and his wife, Baba Kafutshi, with their family in Congo.

Elvina (Neufeld) Martens

Congo. Kafutshi stayed in school one year, then married a fellow student, Kakesa Samuel.

Kafutshi's first pregnancy ended tragically. The baby died, and she nearly did, also. The next child was premature and weighed less than a kilogram at birth. Kafutshi's mother-in-law, a midwife at Mukedi hospital, helped her care for the little one, but Kafutshi's grandmother kept telling her, "Throw that thing away and start a new baby." Kafutshi and her mother-in-law persevered, and the baby survived. Kakesa and Kafutshi had five or six more children.

From 1970 to 1980, Kafutshi, concerned about the Christian family, was a leader in women's work. As president of the Mennonite Women's Society, she was a member of the administrative council for the denomination, and a delegate to the annual General Assembly. In that era men did not appreciate having an African woman on the council, and refused to make travel arrangements for her. When she arrived at the meetings, they put her in charge of the food! Kafutshi arranged everything with her usual efficiency, attended all of the sessions, and to the dismay of the council, expressed her opinions.

Kafutshi and Kakesa were known for their hospitality; dining with them was an experience to remember. Their relationship was close to an ideal marriage. A highlight for Kafutshi was to accompany her husband to the Mennonite World Conference in Curitiba, Brazil, in 1972, and from there, to travel to the United States and Canada to attend the 60th anniversary celebration of Mennonite mission work in Congo.

—*Elvina (Neufeld) Martens*

A WOMAN OF GREAT PRICE

Ashin Tirkey's grandfather, Sirkanti, was baptized by missionary P.A. Penner in 1904—the first leprosy patient to be baptized in the General Conference mission in India. Ashin, not able to live with her infected parents, entered the boarding house at Funk Memorial School in Janjgir. The life of the school's founder, Annie C. Funk, who drowned when the Titanic sank in 1912, inspired young Ashin to become a nurse.

In 1936 Ashin married Benjamin Tirkey, a teacher at Jansen Memorial Higher Secondary School in Jagdeeshpur, and joined the nursing staff of Sewa Bhawan Hospital there.

Ashin worked long hours at the hospital, cared for her family, yard, and house, and entertained guests. On her half-days off, she participated in the women's group of her church. Her husband Benjamin was also active in the church, and served as treasurer of the conference. His favorite pastime was hunting.

Suddenly, Ashin's life was forever changed. On Sunday afternoon, August 3, 1961, Benjamin, trying to retrieve the duck he shot, waded into a pond, got entangled by weeds, and was sucked deep into the mire. Rescuers came too late.

The news of Benjamin's drowning shattered the entire community. Ashin and her sons were helpless with grief, yet her faith and dedication to family, work, and church sustained her. Ashin continued to serve, both through word and deed, at the hospital. In 1977, after 41 years as a nurse, she was honorably retired.

In her retirement, Ashin built a little house next to her well cared-for garden. She never failed to bring the first fruits of her garden to the Lord on Sunday mornings. After the service, the produce was sold by auction, and the money was placed into the church treasury.

—*Helen Kornelsen*

Helen Kornelsen

Ashin Tirkey, the nurse.

FROM DESPAIR TO MINISTRY

Vinit Knox grew up in a loving Christian home in Jagdeeshpur, India. As a child, Vinit participated in a Bible club and memorized 100 Bible verses for the prize of a New Testament, an experience he cherished as an adult.

With a bachelor of commerce degree and 200 rupees for travel and food, Vinit left his parental home in Ambikapur to seek his fortune in Bhopal. His dreams were shattered when his money ran out and he could not find work. He became a homeless beggar and contemplated suicide. Then he remembered happier childhood days in Jagdeeshpur, and the Bible verses he learned comforted him. He read his Bible again, devoted time to prayer, and attended Sunday morning worship services.

After four months of homelessness, Vinit finally found work in a bank, and his life improved. Although he enjoyed his work, God's spirit moved Vinit to dedicate his life to ministry. His evangelistic zeal and effective witness resulted in a call to serve St. John's Church in Bhopal. Eventually he felt called to serve the poor and plant a church designed to meet their needs. With a loan of 300,000 rupees, he acquired a liquor hall and turned it into the City Church of Bhopal. It was dedicated on June 11, 1995.

His ministry expanded to include the Holy Child Care Home, directed by his wife Innis. Poor working parents now had a place to leave their children during the day. Soon the building also housed the Christian Clinic, staffed by 15 doctors who gave free physical examinations.

The congregation continues to contribute toward free medications for the poor. Vinit is in demand as a special speaker in other parts of India. One cloud, however, has hung over Vinit's family since December 2, 1984. Close to where he and his family lived in Bhopal, in an incident reported around the world, a gas leak was discovered at the Union Carbide plant. The disaster affected the health of the entire family, and that of thousands of other local people. Yet, Vinit's zeal and enthusiasm to reach the needy for the Lord are unabated. He is committed to preach the gospel to all who will hear, rich or poor, Hindu or Moslem, but especially to the poor.

—Helen Kornelsen

A Hindu convert being baptized by Pastor Vinit Knox, right, in Bhopal, India.

Helen Kornelsen

40

PUYANG CHURCH REOPENED

Missionaries were forced to leave China in 1941. Clouds of persecution hovered over the country, and nothing was heard of the plight of the Christians for many years.

The church in Puyang (Kaizhou), built by pioneer missionaries Henry J. and Maria (Miller) Brown, closed in 1944, and the building was used for other purposes. In 1993 the church was given back to the people, but it was a mess. The roof leaked so badly that services were canceled whenever it rained. Money for repairs was scarce. The Christians in Puyang asked Mennonite friends in North America to help.

The Commission on Overseas Mission pledged $12,000, and the Chinese Christians were asked to do the rest. Through great sacrifice the people raised $5,000, but that was not enough. These Christians, though poor, prayed, and then the 7,000 believers in Puyang and the surrounding areas began to give. In 50 days they raised an additional $10,000! This was quite a feat when most farmers in the area earn less than U.S. $300 a year.

In 1995 when renovations were completed, the building was rededicated. When the North American guests arrived at the church for the service with $12,000 in their pockets, they discovered that their money was no longer needed. However, the church accepted a gift of money to purchase a piano. The church has since announced plans to build a small Bible training center for the many Christians in the countryside who want to study.

More than 1,000 people attended the four-hour dedication service. Seven hundred crowded into packed benches, and 300 stood in the aisles throughout the service. The overflow was in the courtyard of the former mission school across the road.

In the congregation was a man who spent 15 years in prison because of his faith and association with the Mennonites. Despite poor health, his eyes spoke loudly of what this worship service meant to him.

—*Myrrl Byler*

Gospel Church in Puyang in 1994, built by China missionary Henry J. Brown in 1917. The church could seat 800 people.

Roland Brown

The Gospel Church reopened and rededicated in Puyang, China, 1995.

Myrrl Byler

41

Paul I. Dyck

Two little friends in India.

Orlando Waltner talks to a man in India who was a drunk and terror in his village. He became a Christian and was a changed man.

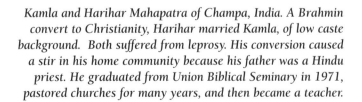

Kamla and Harihar Mahapatra of Champa, India. A Brahmin convert to Christianity, Harihar married Kamla, of low caste background. Both suffered from leprosy. His conversion caused a stir in his home community because his father was a Hindu priest. He graduated from Union Biblical Seminary in 1971, pastored churches for many years, and then became a teacher.

Arthur Thiessen

Mrs. Li Ching Fen was chosen as moderator of the Daming Fu congregation. She was respected by men and women alike.

Wilhelmina Kuyf, with the help of Bible women such as Pauline Wang, ministered in outlying areas of the GC mission in China.

Betty Jean Pannabecker

Hu Sulian grew up in the Mennonite Mission in Puyang. Now a retired dermatologist, she is deeply involved in the Anyang Church. Three thousand people attended the Christmas services in 1994.

Aganetha Fast shared the gospel in villages and out-stations in the countryside in China.

43

Kelendende Lwadi is president of the Mennonite Women of Congo, a deacon and co-pastor of a church, and a Kinshasa seminary staff member.

Peter Rempel, 1994

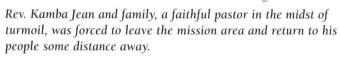

Rev. Kamba Jean and family, a faithful pastor in the midst of turmoil, was forced to leave the mission area and return to his people some distance away.

Frieda Guengerich

Kake Elizabeth's husband left her with seven children. She learned midwifery and cared for her family. She is respected and looked to for Christian counseling by people in the village. In October 1987, Kake Elizabeth was the first woman ordained as a deacon in her area in Congo.

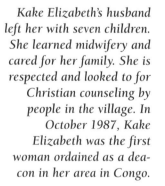

Grace (Hiebner) Harder

44

Poporo, far left, almost failed his studies at Bible school in Congo. He became a courageous, hard working, and successful pastor, covering his territory on foot or by bicycle.

Graduating with highest grades from Bible school in Congo, Tembo Suzanne and her husband Rev. Mwizu, also a graduate, are active in church work.

Jeremiah and Karina Derksen, children of Rick and Marilyn (Carter) Derksen, Congo.

45

BOOM! An explosion rocked the old passenger ship *Zam Zam* on April 17, 1941. Passengers were shaken… then another BOOM! On board were Merle and Dorothy (Bowman) Schwartz, missionaries en route to Congo. It was World War II. The *Zam Zam*, traveling "blackout," was spotted by the enemy. Fifty-five shells demolished the ship and its radio system. No SOS could be sent. Water rushed in. Smoke filled the corridors and stairways. People ran! People screamed! More BOOMS! The Schwartzes made their way to a lifeboat, only to find that it had been destroyed. "Wait for another boat!" yelled an officer. The next lifeboat,

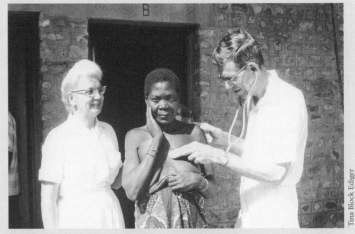

Dr. Merle Schwartz and his wife Dorothy (nurse) were on the Zam Zam when it was torpedoed. Seen here with a patient at Mukedi, Congo, 1971.

they saw was filled only with crew members. The stranded passengers were left behind.

Another search found a lifeboat at the bottom of a swinging rope ladder. Below, the sea was calm. Safe at last, their lifeboat bobbing in the water, and a beautiful rainbow above, the Schwartzes were reminded that God was with them.

Then a ship approached. Was it a friend or foe? A Nazi flag, a swastika, soon told them they were about to become prisoners of war.

In America, family and friends heard that the *Zam Zam* had been torpedoed. After two months, the U.S. government announced that the ship and all its passengers were evidently lost. The Schwartzes were missing and presumed dead.

Shortly after that, however, the German government gloatingly announced that all passengers were safe in France. The memorial service planned by Dorothy's family was canceled and the U.S. government arranged for the Schwartz's travel home. Their family, church, and Congo Inland Mission community joined in thanksgiving to God for bringing the Schwartzes safely through this experience.

—from reports, and *The Hand of the Lord in the Lives of Merle and Dorothy Schwartz*, by Dorothy (Bowman) Schwartz.

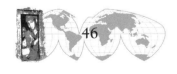

Chapter 2

Mission Expansion After World War II

Colombia, Japan, Taiwan, Uruguay, Mexico

World War II brought mission expansion to a halt. Missionaries were advised not to travel. Some, however, felt the call so strongly that they dared to leave the safety of their homes. At least four General Conference missionary families endured the harsh consequences of that choice.

Dorothy (Bowman) and Merle Schwartz were captured by the Nazis when their boat was torpedoed (see accompanying story). The families of Marvin and Frieda (Albrecht) Dirks, Albert and Wilma (Lichti) Jantzen, and Lester and Agnes (Harder) Wuetrich, en route to America from China, spent three and a half years in prison camps in the Philippines before the U.S. Army rescued them in April 1945.

When World War II ended, millions of people, many of them refugees, were in need of physical aid and hope for the future. Again, Mennonites in North America responded. With renewed hope, dedication, and resources, new ministries were born. The General Conference mission board expanded its programs to Colombia in 1945, and in the 1950s to Japan, Taiwan, Uruguay, and Mexico.

A new reality during this time was the participation of Canadian missionaries. Beginning with the appointment of Anne Penner to India in 1947, the contingency of Canadians has grown to about 40 percent of the COM mission team in 1998.

Colombia

General Conference mission work in Colombia began with an exploratory trip by veteran China missionary W.C. Voth and mission candidate Gerald Stucky. Despite years of Catholic persecution of Protestants, there seemed to be a new openness to

Colombia missionary family in 1948 (l–r, standing): Gerald and Mary Hope (Wood) Stucky, Alice Bachert, Janet Soldner, Arthur Keiser; (middle) Helen (Morrow) Keiser, Harriet (Fischbach) Rutschman; (front) LaVerne Rutschman

Mary (Becker) Valencia and Mary Hope (Wood) Stucky at the 50th anniversary of the Colombia mission on October 1, 1995.

Vernelle Yoder, right, COM missionary, was honored for her years of service to the Colegio Menno in La Mesa. With her is Judith Navarrete, alumni president.

José Chuquin raised the vision of the Colombian Mennonite Church in terms of stewardship and mission. He was the executive director of World Vision for Latin America. During a visit to Lima, Peru, in 1991, he was gunned down. He died five days later in the United States.

48

other groups. The missionaries settled on a campground in the mountains near Cachipay as a place to establish a witness. In 1945, Gerald and Mary Hope (Wood) Stucky, Mary Becker (Valencia), and Janet Soldner (Nussbaum) arrived in Colombia. Two years later, they opened a school for healthy children of

Ordained in 1993, Peter Stucky, son of missionaries Gerald and Mary Hope (Wood), grew up in Colombia and was educated in the United States. He chose to return Colombia, and has dedicated himself to serve the people and the Mennonite church.

In 1997 Marco Güete (center), director of CLARA—the Latin America Anabaptist Resource Center—was interviewed at radio station HCJB and Trans World Radio in Quito, Ecuador. The interviewer was Dairy Rubio, a Mennonite pastor in the city.

Mrs. Arevalo appreciates the home for the elderly in Bogota, founded by Olivia Bastidas with the help of the Mennonite Church in Colombia.

Karen McCabe-Juhnke

Ricardo Pinzon, a law student who refused to serve in the military. He is the director of the Conscientious Objectors' program in Bogotá, Colombia.

Scott Brubaker-Zehr, 1994

People from the Mennonite church helped Edith Cortes set up a small shop in her community. Separated from her husband, she was drawn to the message of love, justice, and respect. She accepted Christ and was baptized.

Edilma Gutierrez Reales, one of the first students at the school near Cachipay, taught and directed the School of Nursing at the National University of Colombia.

parents suffering from Hansen's Disease (leprosy) near Cachipay.

When Mennonite missions began in Colombia, missionaries were in charge of the churches, institutions, and legal matters. At first, the Colombian churches and the mission worked side by side. By 1960 capable Colombian leaders formed the Iglesia Menonita Colombiana (Mennonite Church of Colombia).

In the mid-1960s the mission, as an official organization, was dissolved, and the church took full leadership and responsibility for the work. In 1968 a new constitution, duly registered with the Ministry of Justice in Bogotá, officially turned over all properties held by the mission. Colombian leaders were named to official positions. A good transition is what mission workers from North America envisioned when their work began in 1947. And so it was!

The social conscience of the Colombian Mennonite Church makes a difference in what is known as the most violent country of the world. Its involvement in peace and justice is well-known within the Colombian Church and beyond.

New life recently has come to the churches in Colombia, according to mission workers Marco and Sandra (Garciá) Güete, who direct the Latin America Anabaptist Resource Center with offices in Santafé de Bogotá. Members of the church are starting house churches; others are leaving their home areas in order to spread the gospel. Workers from the Colombian church have established Christian fellowships in new areas of Colombia, in Ecuador, and the United States.

Japan

Japan welcomed help from mission organizations, following its defeat in World War II. The GC mission board had not opened new areas in Asia since 1914, and saw Japan as a place where Mennonites could make a difference. In 1951 W.C. Voth, a "consultant" for the mission board, along with Verney Unruh, a mission candidate, explored possibilities of service in Japan. They selected Miyazaki Prefecture on Kyushu Island as the place to locate. Between 1951 and 1954, 20 missionaries found creative ways to meet the needs of a people deeply hurt by the war. Their main witness was through English classes and friendship evangelism.

In Kobe, in the early 1950s, while missionaries were still in language school, a group of young people requested classes in English and the Bible. The first converts were to become significant church leaders, spiritually dedicated and theologically articulate.

The Japan missionary family in 1953. Standing, (l–r): Verney and Belva (Waltner) Unruh, Peter Voran, Bernard Thiessen, W. C. Voth, Paul Boschman, Ferd Ediger, Viola (Duerksen) Ediger, and Martha Giesbrecht. Seated, (l–r): Lois (Geiger) Voran, Ruby (Siebert) Thiessen, Matilda (Kliewer) Voth, LaVerne (Linscheid) Boschman, Esther Patkau, Leonore Friesen, and Anna Dyck.

Pastors in Japan in the early 1960s (l–r): Hiroshi Isobe, Hiroshi Yanada, Takeomi Takarabe, Verney Unruh, and Yoshichika Miyatani.

Dr. Fujita (left) and Mr. Abe, members of the Baba Cho Church in Kobe. Mr. Abe was drawn to the Christian faith through Verney Unruh's witness.

From the beginning, this mission's goal was to establish independent churches that could take responsibility for evangelism and church development. Since its formation from six congregations in 1965, the Japan Mennonite Christian Church Conference has taken the initiatives to start new work. It invites and assigns missionaries to areas where they will serve. The Kyushu Mennonite churches, though small, have even promoted overseas mission outreach:

Orlando Goering

Pastor Ishiya shares a Bible story with his son and the Tokara children in 1987.

大分メノナイトキリスト教会
集会案内

日 曜　教会学校 ― 朝　9:00
　礼　拝 ― 10:30
曜 祈祷会 ― 夜　7:30
曜 賛美の会 ― 昼　2:00

以上の集会を行っていますぜひおいで下さい。

牧師 佐々木淳二 TEL58-78

Mary (Klassen) Derksen, 1987

Toshiko Oshita (left), a Christian nurse, brought Kimiyo Sato (right), also a nurse, to church. Now Kimiyo is one of the pillars of the Beppu Church in Japan.

Seven-year-old Kusuke Uchida helps 87-year-old Mr. Mitsushita find a Bible passage during the worship service in the home of Peter and Mary (Klassen) Derksen.

Fusae and Toshiko Oshita in Japan. Toshiko became a Christian in the Oita Mennonite Church and, after serving in Malawi, led her mother to faith.

Thirtieth anniversary of GC Mennonite Mission in Japan, 1981.
Front row: Verney Unruh
Middle row (l–r): Ruby (Siebert) Thiessen, Anna Dyck, Lily Derksen, Georgia Liechty, Carl Liechty, Sandra (Cook) Liechty, Belva (Waltner) Unruh, and Fritz Sprunger
Back row (l–r): Alice Ruth (Pannabecker) Ramseyer, Virginia Claassen, Tim Sprunger, Lois (Geiger) Voran, Ellen (Hostetler) Sprunger, Mary (Klassen) Derksen, Robert Ramseyer, Peter Voran, Peter Derksen, and Bernard Thiessen

Robert Ramseyer with a Bible study group that sent contributions to COM in 1992 for the work of John and Tina (Warkentin) Bohn in Lesotho.

Alice Ruth (Pannabecker) Ramseyer

- Miss Chizuko Katakabe joined Mennonite Central Committee in Africa, then became a mission worker to Japanese people living in England. Today she is pastor of the Atago Mennonite Church in Nobeoka, Japan.
- Teruko Yano of the Hyuga church served two terms with MCC in Vietnam.
- The churches supported a Mennonite Church missionary family in Quito, Ecuador.
- The Mennonite congregation of Oita provided partial support for COM missionaries Rick and Marilyn (Carter) Derksen in Congo. Rick, one of its members, is the son of veteran missionaries to Japan, Peter and Mary (Klassen) Derksen.
- Anna Dyck, retired from missionary service in Japan in 1992, helped found a church for Japanese immigrants in British Columbia, and received partial support from a Mennonite congregation in Japan.

"If there had been no other blessing in my 25 years of ministry in Japan, my friendship with Takashi Katsuragi alone would have made it all worthwhile. But there were countless other blessings, and there are many other stories to tell."

—*George Janzen, Japan*

A farewell service was held in Fukuoka, Japan, for Rick and Marilyn (Carter) Derksen from Congo, on a visit to Japan. Pastor Miki led in prayer. Rick is the son of Peter and Mary (Klassen) Derksen, missionaries in Japan.

Mary Derksen, 1993

Virginia Claassen

Mr. Tada, a member of the new Japanese Mennonite Fellowship in Surrey, British Columbia, gave a report on the fellowship to the Sadowara Christian Church in Japan in 1994.

Taiwan

When the Chinese Nationalist government took over the country in 1945, many mission organizations also entered. In 1948 Mennonite Central Committee (MCC), known for its relief work in China, was invited to help. Workers, including Roland and Sophie (Schmidt) Brown, began a medical ministry to aboriginal mountain tribes in 1948.

In 1954 the General Conference sent its first workers, Hugh and Janet (Frost) Sprunger, to Taiwan, and MCC transferred its medical ministry to the mission in 1956. During the next 40 years, 130 other missionaries served, helping the Fellowship of Mennonite Churches in Taiwan (FOMCIT) take root.

The economic boom in Taiwan enabled Mennonite Christian Hospital in Hualien and Mennonite churches to become independent of COM financial subsidy by 1991. Today there are 19 churches in Taipei, Taichung, and Hualien, with a total membership of 1,500.

A major transition for the Mennonite Church in Taiwan happened on February 27, 1994. At the 40th anniversary celebration of FOMCIT, a sister church agreement with the General Conference Mennonite Church of North America was signed. The ceremony marked the dissolution of the General Conference Mennonite mission in Taiwan and the transfer of full responsibility to the church for the continuing ministries of evangelism, church planting, and social service.

Following the closure of the mission, three significant events occurred in the church. It changed its name in Chinese to one that focuses its identity

Verney Unruh, 1987

Dr. Roland Brown, interim administrator of Mennonite Christian Hospital, receives official seals from outgoing administrator M.J. Kao. Sheldon Sawatzky, center, then board chair, officiates.

as a Taiwan church, issued its first public declaration on peace and the destiny of Taiwan, and sent out its first missionary.

The church operates the 500-bed Mennonite Christian Hospital (MCH) in Hualien, which is the

Chaplain Paul Lin and new believer at Mennonite Christian Hospital in Hualien.

largest on the East Coast of Taiwan. MCH cares for the physical and spiritual needs of the sick and, through its ministry, many have found Christ.

The New Dawn Development Center for the developmentally challenged, started by missionaries Otto and Elaine (Ross) Dirks, now directed by FOMCIT, plays a leading role in this area of ministry in Taiwan.

FOMCIT's social conscience led to the establishment of the Good Shepherd Center, a ministry to aboriginal child prostitutes. It received national attention when its leader, Katherine Wu, was attacked by those who wanted to stop her work. The center has received government praise and national attention. (See story on page 81.)

Small group Bible study at pastors', elders', and deacons' retreat in 1982.

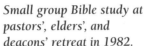

In 1983 Fellowship of Mennonite Churches in Taiwan Treasurer Norman Chien, standing, proposed that FOMCIT become financially independent of COM support within three years.

Verney Unruh

The 40th anniversary celebration of FOMCIT in 1994. At the signing of a sister agreement with GCMC are (l–r): Hugh Sprunger, first COM missionary to Taiwan; Thomas Lehman, COM chair; Larry Kehler, COM secretary for Asia; Titus Liao, FOMCIT secretary; and David Lin, chair of FOMCIT.

On observing the Mennonite Church in Taiwan 40 years after his first arrival in the country, missionary Hugh Sprunger said, "It is amazing to see the relatively small Mennonite Church in Taiwan boldly facing large programs and projects with faith

New Dawn Development Center's new building in 1995, with Otto and Tina Dirks in the foreground. Otto and his late wife, Elaine (Ross) Dirks, founded this institution in 1977.

Dedication of the new 500-bed Mennonite Christian Hospital in Hualien, begun by Dr. Roland Brown in the 1950s. Brown has received national recognition for his sacrificial service.

Fu-An Church women sorting and preparing clothes for Bangladesh in 1981.

Evangelist and Mrs. Wong, early church planters in Taichung. Four of their sons are pastors, one of whom is chaplain to President Lee Tung-hui.

57

Since Taiwanese is a tonal language, a syllable can have various meanings depending on the tone. Missionaries who learn Taiwanese often make glaring mistakes by using the wrong tone. One missionary was preaching about the Sermon on the Mount, and by changing tones, he said that "Jesus was biting to death the people on the mount."

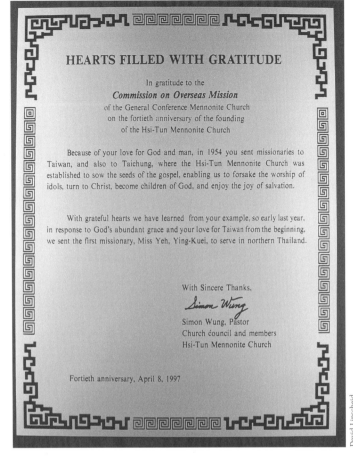

HEARTS FILLED WITH GRATITUDE

In gratitude to the
Commission on Overseas Mission
of the General Conference Mennonite Church
on the fortieth anniversary of the founding
of the Hsi-Tun Mennonite Church

Because of your love for God and man, in 1954 you sent missionaries to Taiwan, and also to Taichung, where the Hsi-Tun Mennonite Church was established to sow the seeds of the gospel, enabling us to forsake the worship of idols, turn to Christ, become children of God, and enjoy the joy of salvation.

With grateful hearts we have learned from your example, so early last year, in response to God's abundant grace and your love for Taiwan from the beginning, we sent the first missionary, Miss Yeh, Ying-Kuei, to serve in northern Thailand.

With Sincere Thanks,

Simon Wung

Simon Wung, Pastor
Church council and members
Hsi-Tun Mennonite Church

Fortieth anniversary, April 8, 1997

David Linscheid

"Hearts Filled With Gratitude" plaque at the 40th anniversary of the Hsi-Tun Mennonite Church.

and confidence. Mennonite churches and work in Taiwan are in good, capable hands! Churches are involved in exciting ways to meet the spiritual, social, and physical needs of people in the church and community."

- When the church in Taiwan became independent of mission support in 1991, it awakened in them a call to be a sending church.
- Carmen and Vincent Chen, a pastor-couple from the Taiwanese Mennonite Church, moved to Argentina to minister to Taiwanese immigrants.
- Some pastors from Taiwan followed their own people to North America, where they planted churches to serve them.
- Since 1996 the Ta-Tung Mennonite Church of Taipei has supported an Indian couple who directs the Village Evangelism and Development Association in Hyderabad, India.
- In 1997 the Hsi-Tun Mennonite Church commissioned Miss Yeh Ying-Kuei as FOMCIT's first mission worker to Thailand.

Evangelist Wung Thian-min is overcome with emotion as he shakes hands with Yeh Ying-Kuei at her commissioning service as FOMCIT's first overseas missionary from Taiwan.

Uruguay

German-speaking Mennonites immigrated to Uruguay after World War II and established three colonies. In 1956, COM and Mennonite Board of Missions (MBM) were involved in starting a seminary in Montevideo to train church leaders for these communities and for the emerging Spanish-speaking churches. Some students went on to plant Mennonite churches in other countries in Latin America and Europe.

In the mid-1970s the seminary closed, and a Mennonite study center was established. Since that time, COM and MBM have provided resources to the study center and have sent short-term workers to train leaders. Through a cooperative organization of the national and German Mennonite churches, COM and MBM also provide grants for evangelism projects and leadership training.

Anabaptist Study Center in Montevideo.

The Emanuel Mennonite Church in Montevideo.

An expression of joy after baptism at Las Piedras in 1986.

59

Mexico

In 1957, COM began a ministry with German-speaking people in the city of Cuauhtemoc, where several thousand Mennonites had emigrated from Canada around 1927. Mission workers served as teachers, medical workers, pastors, and Bible school teachers, and worked closely with the German-speaking congregations at Blumenau, Burwalde, and Steinreich. COM continues to relate to these churches which form the Conference of Mennonites in Mexico. The Mexican conference has mission work among the Spanish-speaking people in the area and sponsors an annual winter Bible school, staffed partly by COM-related workers.

Sunday school class at Anahuac church. At top left is Isaac Bergen, mission worker.

(l–r): Judy Heinrichs, mission worker Helen Ens, Anna Letkeman, and Tina Penner with Pastor Quezada en route to a mountain village.

Bible School at Steinreich, Mexico.

Mexico Festival at Blumenau Mennonite Church, November 1984. Instrumental music by Burwalde Church. COM mission worker Susan Froese is third from left.

John Fehr

Helen Ens

The charter members of the newly founded Eben-Ezer Church in Cuauhtemoc in 1994. Standing (l–r): Alvira Friesen, Mirella Ceniceros, Angelita de Sandoval, Josefina de Rempening, Maria Elena de Millan. Sitting (l–r): Gerhard Walter Rempening, Nicolas Ceniceros, Juan Millan.

IF YOU HAD NOT COME TO JAPAN...

Verney and Belva (Waltner) Unruh arrived in Japan in 1951. After two years of language study in Kobe, they moved to Miyakonojo. One evening Miyatani, a young man, appeared at their door and requested English lessons. A poverty-stricken but eager high school student, he never missed a class. The Unruhs soon realized that Miyatani was thirsty for more than English lessons. He was a true seeker, thirsty for the Word of God. On October 30, 1954, he and another young man were the first to be baptized by General Conference missionaries in Miyakonojo.

After graduating from high school, Miyatani attended Japan Christian College in Tokyo. During vacations he returned to Miyakonojo to help the missionaries. Miyatani continued his education in Europe and in North Africa, where he studied the life and work of Augustine, the great fourth century Christian leader. On a visit to Rome, Miyatani met the Pope.

Having earned his doctorate degree, Miyatani became a professor of church history at a Christian university near Kobe. Today he is considered Japan's authority on Augustine.

In 1991 Miyatani visited the Unruhs in Newton. One night during their devotions, Verney asked him to lead in prayer. Miyatani began with a couple of phrases, then burst into tears. He embraced Verney and said, "If you had not come to Japan, I would not have come to know God, and I would not be where I am today." Little did the Unruhs realize that the teenager in shabby shoes and patched pants would become an outstanding Christian scholar in Japan.

—*Verney Unruh*

Professor Yoshichika Miyatani from Japan with Verney Unruh, former missionary to Japan.

GRACE IN THE MOUNTAINS

Kao Fu-mei, determined and young, dreamed that there was a God who loved her, although she had never heard of him. A Presbyterian evangelist told Fu-mei to go to Mennonite Christian Hospital in Hualien where they "teach about such a God as you are dreaming of."

This hospital operated a school of nursing from 1959 to 1975, training nurses from the island's different cultures and languages. Although Fu-mei was underage, her persistence got her enrolled in the school's first class, along with seven other women. Fu-mei faithfully attended chapel services and studied her Bible. Here she made this God of love her God, and began sharing her faith with enthusiasm. One day missionary Sue Martens and a co-worker, on a trip to the southern tip of Taiwan, found Fu-mei sleeping on a bench in a train station. She had traveled here to preach in a church in the mountains!

Six months before she was to graduate, Fu-mei's parents called her home to prepare for a marriage they had arranged for her. Four months later, however, she returned. She could not marry the man because he was not a Christian. Fu-mei finished her studies and joined the staff of Mennonite Christian Hospital. Before long, she returned to her home village to marry a Christian man.

Three years later Sue Martens and other staff attended the dedication of a new church in Fu-mei's mountain village. Eagerly Fu-mei met them at the nearest station and escorted them to her village, three hours away. During this trek they learned about Fu-mei's life and trials. Shortly after her wedding, Fu-mei had discovered that her husband was not a Christian after all. While he drank in the village, she would pray in the mountains for him. One day when she returned, her husband said, "You win; now I, too, will follow your God." As they walked, Fu-mei said to Sue and the others, "Today he is one of our church leaders, and his faith is much stronger than mine."

—*Susan (Martens) Kehler*

Nurses from Mennonite Christian Hospital singing at worship service of Fu-An Mennonite Church, Hualien, Taiwan, 1987.

FAITHFUL CHOICES

Rosa Triana's husband disappeared during the violence in Colombia in the early 1950s. He was never heard from again. Rosa left the dangerous area and moved with her two small children to La Mesa, where Mennonites had begun a work. Here she met a farmer, moved in, and had five more children.

When Rosa committed her life to Christ, she felt she could not remain in this out-of-wedlock union. The father of her children, however, refused to marry her. She became a homeless mother with seven small children. The church reached out to her in love and practical help.

Rosa, practically illiterate, loved the Bible and educated herself by reading it. She also grew in faith as she sought to live out Christian principles. Church attendance was important, and all her children attended the Mennonite school.

The Poverty Fund, established by General Conference Mennonite churches in North America, made it possible for Rosa to buy a home for her family. Rosa's dreams for a better life were realized when, with a loan from Mennonite Economic Development Associates, she was able to operate a bakery out of her home so that the family could work together. Rosa decided early on not to work on Sundays. She said, "This bakery is a gift from God and belongs to him. We will be faithful to him, and trust him to provide materially during the six days of the week." God blessed the family, and their business thrived.

A strong woman of faith, Rosa is admired and respected by all in her community. Young people come to her for counsel. Her greatest joy is seeing her children follow in her footsteps and faithfully serve God in the church.

—*Margaret (Voght) Ediger*

ABANDONED, BUT NOT FORSAKEN

I came to know the Lord through the early General Conference missionaries while they were still in Japanese language study in Kobe.

I was 17 and the youngest of a study group the missionaries led. I had little interest in the Bible. My purpose was to study conversational English. Tea and homemade cookies also drew me to class. The Lord used my impure intentions for the good, however. One day when I was studying the book of Acts with Peter Voran, I came under conviction. On my way home, I accepted Jesus Christ as my Lord and Savior.

I felt warmth among the people in the small Bible class. Four of us were baptized months later by Peter Voran. That was the happiest moment I ever had.

A couple of weeks later, these missionaries told us the mission had decided to work mainly in Kyushu, and that they did not plan to start a church in Kobe. They encouraged us to find another church. We were shocked and felt forsaken. We felt like unwanted children.

Then we decided to form our own church. The missionaries' garage became our meeting place. From then on, we met by ourselves, and every baptized member started to preach. When it was my turn, I preached from Genesis.

We were all immature. We had no theological education. We knew so little about what it means to be a church, but we nevertheless felt we were one.

Though small and young, we committed ourselves to the Lord and to each other.

Three years later, I went to Tokyo to study. Another original member of the group served a congregation started by that early group of missionaries. Years later, the mission invited me to work in Kyushu, first as a literature worker, then as pastor of congregations started through those same missionaries.

The experiences I had in my earlier years as a Christian have shaped my understanding about the church. It is an autonomous fellowship of believers based on voluntary church membership, and thoroughly dependent on the Lord. I thank the Lord for those good missionaries who helped me grasp this conviction by being faithful to their own sense of call.

—Hiroshi Yanada

Pastor Hiroshi Yanada and his wife Takako on a suspension bridge near Miyazaki.

Glendon Klaassen, 1995

65

MRS. PAN'S GIFT TO THE LORD

Mr. and Mrs. Pan and their children lived in a small fishing village in Meilun, Taiwan. Their house had many cracks in the walls, and they suffered cold winters. Poverty kept them from getting an adequate education. Mr. Pan worked hard at his fishing to meet the family's needs.

The gold bracelet Mrs. Pan gave to the church in Hualien, Taiwan.

Mrs. Pan's gold bracelet provided this pulpit for the Meilun Mennonite Church in Taiwan.

66

Mrs. Pan became a Christian while working in a missionary home. Eagerly she accepted an invitation to join a catechism class. Since she could not read Chinese, she tried to memorize what the teacher said. When it came time to be baptized, however, the evangelist and the pastor decided that Mrs. Pan was not ready; they felt she did not understand Christianity clearly enough. Disappointed, she continued to attend worship services anyway.

When the group of Christians in Meilun outgrew their meeting place, they decided to buy some property and remodel it as a sanctuary and parsonage. Its central location allowed the people to walk or ride a bicycle to church. Though they were poor, everyone was asked to contribute what they could to the remodeling of the building. Gifts also came from the Mennonite churches in Taiwan, from missionaries, and from supporters in North America.

But one special gift, like the widow's mite, overshadowed them all.

Mrs. Pan, who had no money to give, offered the gold bracelet she received as a wedding gift—her "insurance" in case her husband should die. The pastor who had helped make the decision that Mrs. Pan was not ready for baptism, was deeply moved by her sacrifice. The gold was appraised, and the pastor bought it for twice its value. The pulpit and two chairs, paid for by Mrs. Pan's gift, reminded the pastor and evangelist that only God knows the intent and purposes of a person's heart.

Mrs. Pan was one of the first to be baptized in the new church. Her husband was baptized a year later.

—*Peter Kehler*

WITNESS TO THE END

Raquel Fajardo, an influential businesswoman, accepted Christ during Colombia's nationwide Evangelism in Depth campaign in 1968. The next year, Raquel was baptized and joined the Berna Mennonite Church near her home in Bogotá, the capital.

The small Berna church, with about 40 persons in attendance, had been struggling with the slow growth. When Raquel joined, she became a "missionary" role model for others. Because of her influence in the community, she always brought someone new with her to worship services. Soon, others began bringing friends, and attendance grew to 100. Raquel did not take credit, but gave God the glory.

She continued to be a faithful servant of God until the day of her untimely death. Sunday morning, October 18, 1981, Raquel brought two young women to church with her. During the sharing time she stood up, introduced her guests, and requested prayer and help for them. Then Raquel sat down, had a heart attack, and died.

—*Reitha (Kaufman) Klaassen*

General Conference missionaries began the church in Cachipay, Colombia, but through the years many of the members moved to Bogotá to find jobs. In 1962 Gerald and Mary Hope (Wood) Stucky began regular monthly meetings in Bogotá, to follow up their former students. These students formed the core of a new Mennonite congregation organized in 1964 by missionaries Howard and Marlene (Short) Habegger. In 1967 the congregation dedicated a new church building in the Berna district of Bogotá. Pictured here is the Iglesia Evangélica Menonita Central Berna in 1983.

REMEMBERING THE BOMB

On August 6, 1945, when Americans dropped the atomic bomb on Hiroshima, Japan, Mrs. Setsuko Kokubu's life was changed forever. She and her 4-year-old daughter were on an errand early that morning when a blinding flash of light, brighter than a thousand suns, shattered everything around them.

A-bomb survivors Mr. and Mrs. Kokubu in their home with missionary Anna Dyck in 1975.

What followed was terrible: people fleeing from the flames and jumping into the river, faces swollen beyond recognition, and children crying for their parents. Mrs. Kokubu was injured, but her daughter was not. But where was her 8-year-old son Kazuhiko? And where was her husband Tomohiko? Miraculously, their lives were spared as well, but it took two days before the family was reunited.

The Kokubus lost everything, but they still had each other. The family moved to Takajo, where they began a new life. For years they suffered the effects of radiation sickness from the bomb. Another son and daughter were born to them.

"In all our illnesses and troubles, there was always someone who loved and cared," Mrs. Kokubu said. "And we are thankful. Looking back, I cannot help but see how the Lord God led and fulfilled his will in our lives."

Through Mennonite missionaries in Takajo, the Kokubus committed their lives to Christ. They were baptized and became members of the Takajo Mennonite Church—he, in 1964, and she, in 1968.

Reflecting on the A-bomb experience, Mrs. Kokubu said, "We need to tell the world that every year there are still those who are suffering and dying from the effects of the bomb. Unless one has experienced it, one cannot really know the horror of it. This loss of life is so meaningless, without any purpose. It is those who have absolutely no relationship to the war itself who become the innocent victims. War must be abolished at all costs. It is a cursed thing. There must never be a third A-bomb holocaust."

—*Anna Dyck*

SEND GOOBER TO TAIWAN

A radical change was about to take place in the lives of the Kauffman family. Robert and Mary and their teenaged sons James and Tim planned to go to Taiwan for three and a half years.

"Did you ever think of taking Tim's dog, Goober, along?" Tim's Sunday school teacher asked the Kauffmans. No, they replied, then named several reasons why it wouldn't work.

The teacher reminded the parents that Tim was giving up a lot of security to go to a strange place, and that a dog is important to a 14-year-old boy. With Tim's parents' permission, he instigated the "Send Goober to Taiwan" fund as a way of helping to send the Kauffmans to Taiwan.

When the church held a commissioning service for the family, Tim's class, about a dozen eighth-grade boys, brought the Goober bank (a Pringles potato chip can with head, feet, and tail) to the church. It was the first time the church ever commissioned a dog!

Goober, a black dachshund, needed more passport pictures than the Kauffmans did. All travel logistics were worked out, and Goober arrived in Taiwan with his family. After a two-week quarantine, he was allowed to go to his new home.

Goober never appreciated the frequent fireworks that were part of Chinese celebrations, but he liked the garbage truck music blocks away. He recognized the key in the downstairs door and eagerly greeted the boys upon their return home. He was a good icebreaker for visitors, and wonderful with children. To one three-year-old, he was magic; after playing with Goober, the child ate and slept—something he had not done in other strange places.

Was Goober too expensive, or too much trouble? At times, Goober was a costly nuisance, but usually he played his role as missionary dog with great skill. In the end, the Kauffmans were glad the church was willing to commission him.

—*Robert and Mary (Fisher) Kauffman*

69

MARIA'S DREAMS COME TRUE

For Maria Dyck, growing up in an Old Colony Mennonite village in Mexico, in the 1960's, the future seemed bleak. She hoped to become a teacher

Maria (Dyck) and Isaac Bergen.

some day, but that was not an option for young women in this very conservative community. Instead, Maria found herself at home with her parents, doing household chores. Evenings were boring, with nothing to do. She would have read books, but they were not available to her.

Maria's father, an elected minister in the Old Colony Mennonite Church, found no joy in his assignment. He could not come to terms with the stringent rules set by the elders of the congregation. He was not allowed to preach the teachings of Jesus in the New Testament. This was against church policy.

The Dyck family heard about a school at Quinta Lupita. First, Maria's brothers were allowed to attend. Then Maria, 19 years old, joined them. She advanced very rapidly in her studies. Maria finished her elementary and high school education in four years and realized her dream to become a teacher. She learned to play the piano, and often accompanied the singing for the church school. Then she taught others to play.

When a teacher was needed at Steinreich, Maria got the job. While there, she married Isaac Bergen. Isaac was an enthusiastic Christian who shared his faith with others. Isaac and Maria took further training at the Mennonite Seminary in Asuncion, Paraguay, and returned to Mexico to serve their people. They helped found two congregations at Anahuac and Cuauhtemoc, and began a witness among the Tarahumara Indians in the mountains.

—*Betty (Schmidt) Epp, Jake and Ella (Klassen) Neufeld, and Abe and Hanna (Vogt) Rempel*

BUILDING TRUST IN A NEW ENVIRONMENT

Ferd and Viola (Duerksen) Ediger lived in a large rented house in the middle of a tree nursery in Hyuga, Japan. Since they were at the edge of town, they raised a few animals to supplement their income. As new missionaries, however, their language skills left a great deal to be desired, especially in the local dialect. They found it difficult to build trusting relationships with neighbors, particularly the Soto family.

One day, Mr. Soto's sow gave birth to 14 baby pigs. Then suddenly, after a few days, she refused to give the babies milk. What to do? They might all die! Such a big financial loss!

In desperation, Mr. Soto asked the Edigers if they could help. Before they left for Japan, the Edigers had been told that any skill, any experience, any training they had could be used in the Lord's work.

Thankfully, Ferd remembered from his growing-up years on a Saskatchewan farm that when a sow refuses to suckle her babies, it is because their new teeth are causing the mother a lot of pain. Mr. Soto promptly produced a pair of pliers, and Ferd pulled out the baby pigs' new little eye teeth. Presto! All was well again. No one was happier than Mr. Soto.

Through the ensuing years, Mr. Soto was a committed member of the Mennonite church and witnessed to others of his faith. Ferd and Viola were thankful that, in their new life in Japan, God could use ordinary experiences and knowledge of the past to bring glory to God's name.

—*Viola (Duerksen) Ediger*

Ferd Ediger milking a goat in Japan.

BY GOD'S GRACE I AM WHAT I AM

When political violence in Colombia displaced my mother and her seven children, the people of Cachipay welcomed us. My mother wanted to educate all of her children but only sent my older sister to school. Finally, I was able to go to a boarding school near Cachipay. I was bright, did well in sports, but got into a fight and was punished. I escaped, and returned to my family.

In October 1960, rebellious and unsettled, I left home again. Three months later, I wrote to my mother. She informed me of a grave misfortune in

Victor Vargas Torres and his wife Blanca in 1998.

the family. Anxious, I returned to Cachipay only to hear that my sister had died. During my absence, mother had become a Christian through the witness of Gerald and Mary Hope Stucky. We began to attend the Mennonite Church in Cachipay.

At 16, I started school at the Colegio Americano in Cachipay, where the Stuckys and Hulda Myers (Weiss Friesen) were my teachers. Here, I accepted Christ as my Lord and Savior. My family is grateful to God for the Colegio Americana. In 1970, after teaching in mission schools in La Mesa and Cachipay for two years, I moved to Bogotá to work and complete studies in accounting.

Through help from the Commission on Overseas Mission, I continued my education in Ibague and received a bachelor's degree. During this time, missionaries Glendon and Reitha (Kaufman) Klaassen, and Armando and Eunice Hernandez established a Mennonite congregation in Ibague.

In 1973, while in Ibague, I married Blanca Rosa Garzón from Cachipay. Our home is blessed by God with four precious children. Today we attend Venga tu Reino (Thy Kingdom Come Church), a daughter congregation of the Mennonite Church of Teusaquillo, which began in our house in 1993.

I am grateful to God for the Mennonite work that introduced me to the gospel of Jesus Christ, and for his servants who carried the message of salvation to Cachipay, Anolaima, and La Mesa. I am grateful to my mother for the sacrifices she made, so that I could study.

—*Victor Vargas Torres, lay leader in the Colombian Mennonite Church*

LAVISH GIFTS—RECEIVED AND GIVEN

Mr. Hwang, co-owner of a printing operation in Taipei, Taiwan, worked seven days a week. As part of the business practice in Taiwan, he and his partner often entertained customers with an evening of "wine, women, and song."

He lived near the Ta-Tung Mennonite Church, which his wife and children attended faithfully. When evangelistic services were held in the church, Mrs. Hwang persuaded her husband to go with her. He was intrigued by the message. Before the week was over, he committed his life to Jesus Christ.

Mr. Hwang's new life conflicted with that of his partner, and he lost his business. Yet his faith and trust in God was not shaken. He began his own business, and prospered. During the next 10 years he helped six young men from the Mennonite Church establish their own printing operations.

He grew in his Christian faith, and was elected first to the church council and then as a deacon. When his family moved to another part of the city, and travel to the Ta-Tung church became difficult, they asked that a second church be established in their area.

Mr. Hwang took out a second mortgage on his home in order to help purchase a church and parsonage for the newly formed Sung-Chiang Mennonite Church.

Mr. Hwang helped the pastor reach out to the community and persuaded others, including women and youth, to get involved in the church. He arranged tours to Mennonite churches in Hualien and Taichung to help the members feel they belonged to a caring fellowship. He also led the congregation in purchasing another facility costing more than U.S. $500,000. At the 20th anniversary of the church, he proposed that the Sung-Chiang Mennonite Church establish and support a new church in another part of the city. This, he felt, was an appropriate way to give thanks for all that God had done for them.

Today, at age 65, this faithful servant has passed many responsibilities to younger adults, so they, too, can experience the joy of serving the church.

—*Peter Kehler*

Elder Hwang Tong-Huei (in white shirt) in Taiwan.

Tina Block Ediger, 1979

73

Healing from the Inside Out

"Get back into bed," thundered Dr. Nakamura as he entered the room. "How do you expect to get well if you don't rest?"

"But I am healed," replied Dr. Fusayasu, as he literally danced around the room with joy. "I'm well. I've been healed!"

"No one gets over your type of kidney disease without seven months' treatment, and you've been here only a week." Dr. Nakamura forced Dr. Fusayasu back into bed.

"All right, I'll stay in bed, but you must examine me to see if I'm well or not," agreed Dr. Fusayasu, as he settled down.

For the next three days, the nurses and staff ran all the tests possible. To their surprise, they found that Dr. Fusayasu was indeed healed! A humbled and bewildered Dr. Nakamura wanted to know what happened. When Dr. Fusayasu came to the hospital, he was a very sick man. If treatment had not been started immediately, he would have died before long.

"How is it that there is no sign of your kidney disease now?" asked the doctor.

Dr. Fusayasu, a busy and famous dentist in Nichinan City, a lay leader in the Japanese "Seicho no Ie" religion, told him this story: Grace-love Christian Kindergarten, started in 1955 in Nichinan, was close to the Fusayasu family residence. Because of its excellent reputation, Dr. Fusayasu wanted his children to attend this kindergarten. Mrs. Fusayasu became good friends with the teachers, and was asked to join the parent-teacher association. Soon, she became a believer. For four or five years, Dr. Fusayasu read the Bible and the stories the children heard in class.

During this time, he became ill with kidney disease, and entered into a deep depression. One day when his wife and a kindergarten teacher visited him in the hospital, he turned his back on them. They left a magazine, *Gospel for the Millions*, on his bedside table. He regretted not having spoken to his beloved wife. He picked up the magazine and read, "My God has never failed me yet!" What striking words! The article convicted him of his own sinfulness, and he confessed his belief in Jesus Christ. Dr. Fusayasu felt the joy of forgiveness and newness of life in Christ.

"Dr. Nakamura," he said, "as I confessed my belief in Jesus as my Savior, I became aware of a warm hand on my shoulder. It began to move down my body until it rested above my kidney. In that moment I knew that not only did the Lord remove my sins from me and give me new life, he also healed my diseased kidney! Yes, Dr. Nakamura, I am healed by the power of my risen Lord Jesus Christ."

In October 1960, Dr. and Mrs. Fusayasu, along with Dr. Nakamura, who also became a believer, were baptized with two other people at a joyous church service. Today, Dr. Fusayasu's family are pillars in the Aburatsu Christian Church (Mennonite) and community. He has shared his testimony with many others, especially with doctors and dentists of various medical associations.

—*Peter Voran*

Dr. and Mrs. Fusayasu and family in Japan.

Peter Voran

FAITH SPARKED BY AN ENGLISH CLASS

Little did I realize what changes would come into my life in 1955, when the first Mennonite missionaries arrived in Montevideo, Uruguay. As a bilingual secretary, I needed to improve my knowledge of commercial English, so I asked one of the missionaries for help. The missionary saw an opportunity to relate to persons who might help form a church happily obliged. I can't remember if I ever paid for those lessons!

Soon the commercial English classes were changed to Bible studies. Raised in the Roman Catholic Church, I was confronted by biblical principles I had not thought about before. The book *Menno Simons: His Life and Writings*, by H.S. Bender and John Horsch, helped me to define my identity as a Mennonite.

There were many things I could not understand or accept. Wisely, the missionary pastor continued to guide me, and eventually I decided to pursue faith and ministry in the Mennonite Church. I was the first person to be baptized by the Mennonite missionaries.

I enrolled in Bible and theological studies at Mennonite Seminary in Montevideo, then at the Associated Mennonite Biblical Seminary in the United States, and at the Study Center of the Mennonite Churches in Uruguay. My desire to explore and discover the riches in the Scriptures has not waned.

Later, I was invited to collaborate full-time in the library of the Mennonite Seminary in Montevideo, and to complete my studies as a librarian. Although the seminary closed its doors in 1974, I continue my ministry as the coordinator for the study center, and serve half-time as general editor for the Mennonite World Conference in the area of communications.

The momentum for God in my life has never slowed.

—*Milka Rindzinski*

Milka Rindzinski (left) and her friend Beatriz Barrios in Montevideo, Uruguay.

"SHE IS OUR MARIA"

Maria Giesbrecht dreamed of becoming a nurse. She was the eldest child and grew up on an Old Colony Mennonite farm in Mexico. Her father owned and operated a small cheese factory, a corner store, and a mixed farm. While the male members of the Giesbrecht family worked the factory and the store, Maria was in charge of the farm, and helped in the garden and kitchen.

Maria's dream would not leave her. She wanted to train to be a nurse at the school where I taught in nearby Cuauhtemoc. Just before classes were to begin, Maria visited me. She was in tears, because her father would not permit her to come, he felt she was too stupid. I convinced Mr. Giesbrecht that Maria was intelligent and would pass the required test with honors. He consented, reluctantly.

Maria, the only Mennonite in the class, was an exceptional student. She was eager to learn, and served willingly. Her stability in her spiritual faith and her love for people inspired all. After a year of intense training, Maria graduated. Her parents attended the graduation celebration and were proud of their daughter's accomplishments.

Maria became a nurse. Months later, Maria's father was diagnosed with lung cancer. Maria left her nursing position in a clinic to care for him at home, day and night. The family was amazed at what she was able to do.

Several years later, Maria became the staff director of a Cuauhtemoc nursing home, whose guests were elderly, malnourished street people, unaccustomed to any routine. Establishing order consumed much of her energy and emotional resources. Maria's perseverance and kindness won her respect and love from every guest in the home. Occasionally, I teased the guests by saying, "Where is *my* Maria?" Their response was always the same: "She is not *your* Maria, she is *our* Maria, and you may not take her away!"

During the two-and-a-half years Maria was at the nursing home, she enriched the lives of all who entered there. Once, during the visit of an evangelist, a guest said that if Maria was going to heaven, he wanted to go there, too. A loud "yes, me too" echoed throughout the audience.

—*Tina Fehr*

Student nurses and missionaries: (l–r) Martha Ayala de Lopez, Margaret Dyck, Adela Salazar, Guillermine Miramontes, Maria Giesbrecht, and Tina Fehr in 1980.

76

FOLLOWING A CALL

When Anna Dyck entered the hospital room of a tuberculosis patient in Miyakanojo, Japan, she found him reading the New Testament. Takeomi Takarabe was searching for meaning in life. On medical leave from the bank, he feared he would lose his job if he did not recover within a limited time. Before long, he committed his life to Christ.

Two years later, with health restored, Takarabe was a baptized member of the Namiki Mennonite Church. Now he had to decide whether to return to his job at the bank or obey God's call to Christian service. He decided on the latter, and left to attend Japan Christian College in Tokyo.

On Takarabe's first summer vacation from school, he returned healthy and happy. He was confident he had met the right girl. Her name was Michiko Onitsuka, a believer who taught in a Christian kindergarten in Tokyo. Takeomi Takarabe and Michiko Onitsuka were married in 1965, and he immediately pastored the Atago Church in Nobeoka. Their home was blessed with two children.

On October 5, 1986, Michiko died of cancer. She was loved and respected by many people—always cheerful, uncomplaining, willing, kind, and caring, just spreading love around. Though there were many tears at her funeral, there was an atmosphere of victory.

Pastor Takarabe is now retired but continues to be actively involved in the Atago Church.

—*Anna Dyck*

Michiko (Onitsuka) and Takeomi Takarabe of the Atago Mennonite Church, Nobeoka, in 1983.

77

A BUDDHIST MOTHER'S VOW

Kim Chen grew up in a Buddhist home in Taiwan. At the age of 1, he became acutely ill with polio, with little hope for survival. His mother sought help from various deities, but to no avail. She had heard about Jesus, and in desperation begged him to help. If her son would live, she promised to dedicate him to God. Kim improved but never recovered the full use of his legs. As he improved, his mother did not forget her vow. Kim grew up with his mother's love and support constantly surrounding him, but never learned the reason for his miraculous healing.

Kim left home to go to high school. Away from his mother's constant care, he suffered terribly from an inferiority complex. His grades dropped, and severe depression set in. Quitting school was not an option; he knew he needed an education to make a living.

Then Kim met some members of the Inter-School Christian Fellowship at his school. He attended the ISCF meetings, and began to read the Bible. Kim gave his life to Christ, and a radical change took place in his thinking. He felt loved and valued by God and people other than his parents. Gradually he overcame his inferiority complex, and could laugh when he fell down.

He told his parents about his new commitment. Their quiet acceptance surprised him. When he decided to be baptized, they finally told him of his mother's vow.

Kim was eventually called to ministry and enrolled in the China Evangelical Seminary. It was here that Kim learned about Mennonites. In addition to library research, he spent some time visiting with Mennonites in Hualien. While completing his studies, the Meilun congregation called him to be their pastor.

At seminary, he met and wanted to marry Cherry Wu. She grew up in a poor Buddhist family and her parents objected to the marriage. After Kim went to the Meilun church in 1988, the congregation joined him in praying for Cherry's parents' permission for their marriage. Finally, the mother gave her approval. After further negotiations, her father grudgingly granted permission for the marriage, but refused to attend the wedding.

Kim and Cherry keep busy and happy with Sunday school, youth work, preaching and teaching, holding prayer meetings, and visiting the sick and elderly.

—*Helen Willms-Bergen*

Cherry Wu and Pastor Kim Chen with daughters Anna and Hanna in Taiwan.

Glendon Klaassen, 1995

NOT YET READY

"Could you make us a wooden cross for our worship services?" I asked Mr. Otoshi during a meeting at the Hiroshima Mennonite Church. Otoshi, a craftsman in wood, attended the home meetings regularly. He asked me if his offer was appropriate since he had not yet made a commitment to Jesus Christ. At the same time, all of the Christians in the room nodded their heads, almost as if they were one body. "Of course, it is," they agreed.

In Hiroshima, explained the group, the church met in the homes of members. Since it was sometimes difficult to feel worshipful in one's own home, a cross could be helpful. After discussing the dimensions of the cross, Mr. Otoshi agreed to do it.

The woodworker was one of the kindest people I had ever met. He loved discussion groups, and invariably put himself in the place of any underprivileged person who might be involved, speaking from that point of view. Others often said, "I never thought of it from that angle."

Three weeks later, at an evening meeting, Mr. Otoshi brought two beautiful crosses, each about 18 inches high, made of fragrant camphor wood. Sanded to a satin finish and unlacquered, the wood seemed alive. The base, a slice of a branch of camphor, gave the illusion of a hilltop.

After the group sat for a time, drinking in the beauty of the crosses, Mr. Otoshi gave a four-inch cross to each of the 17 members. All were made from the same piece of wood. Finally he pulled out a

A baptismal worship service in the home of Robert and Alice Ruth (Pannabecker) Ramseyer in Hiroshima, Japan, 1992. The cross was made by Mr. Otoshi.

Robert Ramseyer

small box with a glass cover. Inside was a small cube of the camphor. He liked what church people said and did, he explained, although he was not ready to call himself a Christian. From his point of view, it would be presumptuous to make himself a cross since he had not made a public confession of faith. Wanting to be a part of this experience, he'd made the cube for himself. By the time he was finished speaking, the group was near tears.

It was very important, said Mr. Otoshi, that all the crosses were made from the same branch. It was a symbol of the "one body," the church of Christ.

—*Alice Ruth (Pannabecker) Ramseyer*

A VOICE FOR THE POOR

Ricardo Esquivia's story is one of rags to riches and then, due to Christian convictions, a voluntary return to poverty. He now works among and on behalf of people experiencing injustice. This commitment forced him to flee his country for a while.

Esquivia was born into a poor peasant family in Colombia's highlands. When the government interned his leprotic father in a leper colony, Ricardo's mother and her four children were left in even tighter economic straits.

Ricardo was able to attend school with hundreds of other children through the help of the Mennonite mission. Eventually he graduated from the External University of Colombia with a degree in law, specializing in human rights.

Ricardo became well established in his practice, and earned good money. But when he realized his employer was involved with the drug market, he left. "I couldn't sleep that night," Ricardo recalls. "I realized that providing airplanes to drug traffickers was no better than selling drugs myself. I talked to my wife and told her I couldn't continue in my job."

The couple moved from Bogotá to San Jacinto on the Caribbean coast, where they worked among a group of peasants, sharing their economic hardship. Ricardo soon understood how local landowners abused the peasants, and decided to use his law degree on their behalf. His action placed him in great danger, and led to death threats. He was even accused as one of the assassins of a Spanish priest.

At the urging of the Colombian Mennonite leaders in 1993, Ricardo spent four months in exile in the United States. After two months, his wife Patricia and two children joined him. The family returned to Colombia after the government cleared his name, but Ricardo continues to live in fear. In spite of this, he pleads the cases of those suffering injustice.

In 1989 Ricardo worked with the Colombian Mennonite Church to begin Justapaz, a peace and justice ministry which trains congregations in nonviolent conflict resolution, a skill especially needed in communities wracked with terror.

—*MCC and GCMC news releases,*
and Tina Block Ediger

Ricardo Esquivia, left, and Cesar Moya, both leaders in the Colombian church.

Frank Soto Albrecht, 1994

A LIFE ON THE LINE

Following several years of pastoral ministry in Hualien, Taiwan, Katherine Wu embarked on a dangerous new ministry. Deeply moved by the many young girls who were sold by their parents into a life of prostitution, Katherine established and directed the Good Shepherd Center, a refuge for child prostitutes. One day, right in front of the home, she was attacked and beaten by persons upset with her interference in the prostitution trade. Hardly able to move, Katherine rang the doorbell just before she became unconscious.

While recovering at Mennonite Christian Hospital, Katherine was visited by the premier of Taiwan, who happened to be in Hualien that day. His visit made headlines all over the island, and a crusade against child prostitution began.

Partly as a result of this publicity, and through her fearless advocacy, Katherine raised enough financial support to purchase a sixth-floor apartment where the girls and their caretakers can live in safety. Seeing the change in the girls' lives and knowing that each one is important to God is reward enough for Katherine.

—*Martha (Boschman) Vandenberg*

Pastor Katherine Wu with husband Lu Hsin Hsiung and daughters Jessica and Fuan in Hualien, Taiwan, 1995.

Chris Leuz

MY FAVORITE JAPANESE GRANDMOTHER

I remember visiting my favorite Japanese grandmother, Ai, over green tea. Grandmother was born in Kagoshima around the turn of the century. Her parents became Christians and gave their children Bible names. One sister was called "The Way," another

Martha (Giesbrecht) Janzen, at left, with Grandma Ai Maruta (holding cake) at her 92nd birthday celebration in Japan.

George Janzen, 1993

"Truth," and her own name was Ai, meaning "love."

She was 89 when I first met her. Ai loved to sing hymns, and her favorites were all marked in the book. The ones she loved best were songs about heaven, a place she was ready to go to.

Ai spoke proudly of the seven doctors in her family, including grandchildren. She could call any one of them for advice when she needed it, but it was her 70-year-old brother-in-law, a doctor, who cared for her. Her daughter Emiko, a committed Christian, was a faithful member of the Takajo Christian Church.

My husband George and I were in our final week in Japan when Ai became critically ill. Friday morning, two days before we were to leave, Ai died. Emiko asked us to conduct the funeral later that afternoon. According to Buddhist tradition, however, Saturday was an "unlucky day" for funerals. The funeral had to be on Friday.

Amid packing and telephone calls, there was no time to prepare for the service. In desperation, George committed himself and the service to the Holy Spirit.

Ai's house was filled to overflowing with family members and friends. For the great majority of those in attendance, it was probably their first experience of a Christian funeral service. By the inspiration of the Holy Spirit, this final major act in the community turned into a rich blessing, perhaps the most effective outreach to the community in our entire four years of ministry. The family expressed its gratitude over and over.

—*Martha (Giesbrecht) Janzen*

OPEN HOMES, NEW CHURCHES

Anita Dyck de Rodríguez was born into an Old Colony Mennonite family near Cuauhtemoc, Mexico. Because her father did not agree with the church's teaching, however, her family became estranged from their community and had to find work among the native Mexicans.

As a young woman, Maria heard of the work of the General Conference Mennonite Church. Her faith was renewed as she learned to know missionaries Tina Fehr, a nurse, and Helen Ens, a teacher. Maria desired to share the love of Jesus with her family and the Mexican children living around her in the town of Anahuac.

Though her home was small and sparsely furnished, Maria invited Helen and Tina to conduct Spanish Bible classes. The many children who came more than filled the space, so another room was rented.

The Mennonite Church of Cuauhtemoc caught Maria's vision and voted to purchase a three-room house in Anahuac to be used as a church and outreach center. This was the first time the congregation was willing to cooperate in a mission to neighboring Mexicans. To this day, the congregation's youth and service groups help in this weekly outreach.

The mission in Anahauc introduced others to Christianity. Magdalena Ceniceros, a native Mexican wife and mother, opened her home for Bible studies and became a pillar in the Anahauc church. Then, for health reasons, the family left Anahauc and moved to a worker housing complex in Cuauhtemoc. Again they opened their home to those who wanted to hear the gospel. A Bible study and Sunday school sprung up. The group eventually became the Eben-Ezer congregation.

Magdalena died of leukemia before she could witness a major milestone in the life of the new congregation: the dedication of its new chapel in the mid 1990s. Magdalena's husband and youngest daughter, however, became charter members.

—*Helen Ens and Betty (Schmidt) Epp*

Magdalena Ceniceros and daughter Irelia.

Helen Ens, 1997

Anita Rodriquez (front left) with members of the new Mennonite Church in Anahuac, Mexico.

To Open or Close Doors?

"Pastor Voran, you need to stop the Naoko Kojima wedding plans. She is a Christian and cannot marry Toru Nishimori, a non-Christian." My wife Lois and I had just arrived in Japan to work with the Hyuga Christian Church, and this was one of the first issues the leadership team presented to us.

I had several meetings with the family and the couple. Finally, after much prayer, it was decided to go ahead with the wedding. Naoko's family and Toru, the husband-to-be, promised not to interfere with Naoko's faith and participation in the church. I explained to the congregation that if they allowed the marriage to take place in the church, it could open the door for the entire family to become believers. After all, Naoko's younger sister was already coming to Sunday school. If the church refused to grant permission, the couple would get married anyway.

Both families and many friends came for this Christian service. The church members welcomed the people and made all feel comfortable.

The welcome continued when they next attended on New Year's Day. Early in the morning, most Japanese visit shrines and/or temples just to make sure the gods will look with favor upon them during the coming year. Christian believers often meet in the morning, eat breakfast together, then share how the Lord led them the past year, and what their dreams and aspirations are for the new year.

Shortly after the service began at the Hyuga Christian Church, the entire Kojima family, along with Toru and Naoka, entered the church. The Kojimas and Toru listened intently as Christians shared what Jesus meant to them. Naoko again thanked the people for allowing her and Toru to get married in the church.

But another dilemma faced us: communion. How would the Kojimas and Toru feel if they were excluded? I felt led to explain the meaning of the bread and cup. Then I told the family and Toru that if they could thank God for Jesus, whom Naoko believed and served, they could also partake in this sacred meal. They all did, and it seemed like a blessed time.

The Kojimas soon began to attend church. Before the year passed, Mr. Kojima and his youngest daughter were baptized, then Mrs. Kojima and a son who worked in Tokyo. Toru, the elder son of the Nishimori family, could not be baptized until after his mother's death but participated in the church services whenever possible.

At their baptisms, Mr. Kojima testified that he came to church because of the "open door" he found there—first, at the wedding of his daughter, then on New Year's morning. Mrs. Kojima testified to the peace of heart and mind she now had in believing in the *living* Lord Jesus Christ. How different from her god shelf, paper prayers, food offering, and candles!

—Peter Voran

Naoka Kojima and Toro Nishimori on their wedding day in April 1979.

Peter Voran, 1979

84

BAPTISM

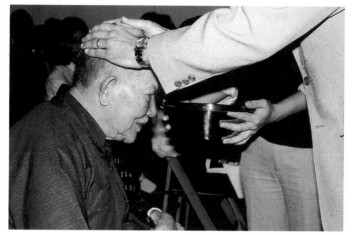

At the age of 85, Mr. Liu became a Christian and was baptized in Hong Kong, 1985.

Jean (Kliewer) Isaac

Rev. J. Koti, baptizing a believer in South Africa in 1991.

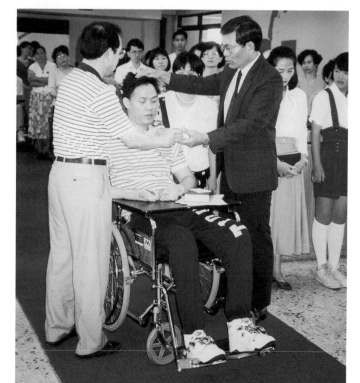

Cármen Miñino, J. Mark Frederick and Vincente Miñino share in the baptism of Rosa in Mexico City, 1995.

Chwei Tzu-Ping being baptized by Pastor Simon Wung at Hsi-Tun Mennonite Church in Taiching, Taiwan, in 1993.

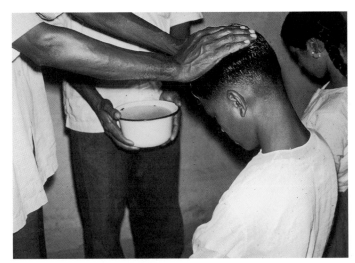

Baptism of youth in India.

Tomoko Koga, left, the first to be baptized at the new Fukuoka Church in Japan in 1991, receives a bouquet from Satoru Hara. Fukuoka Church was started by Peter and Mary Derksen.

Mary (Klassen) Derksen

Pat and Rad Houmphan conduct a baptism in Thailand, 1997.

PREACHING THE WORD

Gerald J.A. Neufeld, 1995

Claire and Siaka Traoré, church leaders in the Mennonite Church in Burkina Faso, 1995.

Tig Intagliata, 1988

Leonidas Saucedo preaches at a membership service in the Heroes del Chaco congregation, Bolivia, April 1988.

Thomas Lehman, 1994

Daniel Ngai, pastor of Grace Mennonite Church, Hong Kong.

Leland Voth, 1996

Evangelist Zhang Wan-xiang in Daming, China is often referred to as Levi because his mother committed his life to God before he was born.

Roland Brown, 1994

Zhang Bao-shan from Puyang, China, spent three years in "education by labor" during the Cultural Revolution. Today Zhang is a leader in the Gospel Church in Puyang, a successful businessman and a county political representative for all religions.

Education

John Bohn and agricultural students at Thaba Khupa, Lesotho, 1980.

James Juhnke

Lois Luez

A physical therapy session at the 1996 dedication of New Dawn Development Center's new building in Taiwan.

Frank Soto Albrecht, mission worker in Colombia, found clowning an effective way to teach mediation skills to adults and children.

88

Children from La Mesa school in Colombia participate in a mediation training session.

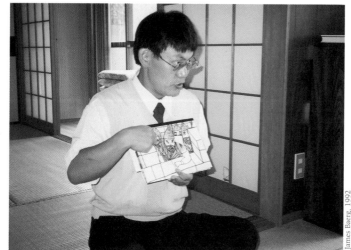

Hisatomi Hashimoto, teaches Sunday school in Oita, Japan. He makes his own picture books to accompany his lessons.

Wendy Choi helps primary pupils with their studies at the Helping Hands Centre in Hong Kong in 1989.

PROJUSE is a voluntary service program for Bolivian youth. This library is where some of the youth have served.

Dennette Alwine, worker with the China Educational Exchange, works with a sophomore English student during a writing workshop.

The Umtata Women's Theological Group evaluates Bible studies in Transkei.

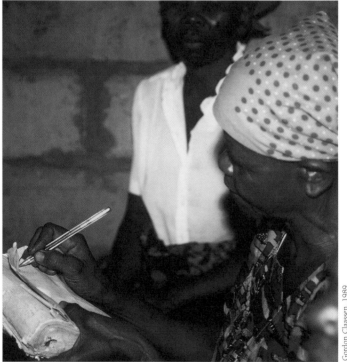

Women taking notes at a seminar in Congo.

Participants in a Bible class conducted by Don Rempel Boschman in Gaborone, Botswana, 1995.

Erwin Rempel

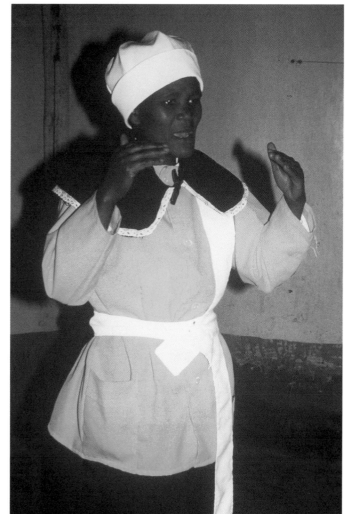

Vivian Luyenge of Transkei.

Jean (Kliewer) Isaac

91

Dukni Bai, an outstanding Bible woman in her day, sings a solo at Korba, India. At 85 she is still praising God.

Special music by Jesus and Lupe Manuel of the Anahuac Church in Mexico.

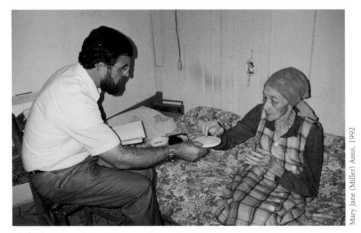

Nilson Assis shares communion with a woman in Ponta Grossa, Brazil.

Ana Maria Belmont in prayer at a Coyoacan Growth Group meeting in her home.

Missions Sunday at the Fukuoka church in Japan when Congo missionaries Rick and Marilyn (Carter) Derksen and their children visited in 1993. The congregation is doing the offering Congolese style by singing and clapping as they take their offerings forward.

Worship in a village congregation in Bolivia.

CEMTA all-school choir singing in Asuncion Mennonite Church, May 4, 1989. Ben Pauls is the conductor.

Silvia de Perez, Daniel Colina and Eduardo Perez direct the singing for a Sunday worship service at Bethel Mennonite Church in Las Piedras, Uruguay.

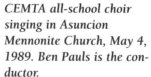

Janjgir youth choir sings at the Bharatiya Mennonite Conference sessions in Janjgir, India, 1987.

Dr. Roland Brown with Taiwan's President Lee Tung-hui on his second visit to Mennonite Christian Hospital, in April 1993.

Glendon Klaassen, COM Latin America secretary, meets with the church council of Argentina's Taiwanese Mennonite Church, 1992.

Lucia Maria do Nascimento, a strong leader in the church in Brazil, was miraculously healed of cancerous growths in her arm. Final x-rays before surgery indicated that the cancer was gone.

Dan Graber, 1988

Archbishop Israel Motswasele (right) of the Spiritual Healing Church in Botswana, attending the Kuhrman Consultation in 1997.

Angela (Albrecht) Rempel

Gladys (Klassen) Buller, 1993

Manango Louise Gisodi, evangelist among women in Congo.

Photo: Frank Soto Albrecht

Responding to the violence in the military, people prepared banners for a demonstration sponsored by JUSTAPAZ, the Mennonite peace office in Bogotá, Colombia, 1994.

Abe and Hanna (Vogt) Rempel

Recording stories for a children's radio program in Cuauhtemoc, Mexico.

Garry Prieb, 1995

Kwekpiri Watara and others listen to translations of Bible stories in Burkina Faso. Kwekpiri had been a tester during the translation process.

Mary (Klassen) Derksen

Missionary Bill Derksen, volunteered to be a translator at the Oita International Wheel Chair Marathon, in Japan, 1992.

95

Women at Miabi, in Congo.

A woman in Lesotho.

Marte Tiera of Burkina Faso, a faithful witness.

Maria Wall and her daughter Trina Titow, immigrants to Germany from Russia. Maria was baptized on April 21, 1996. An effective children's worker and storyteller both in the Russian and German languages, she wants to spread the love of Jesus to others.

Joshua, son of Gordon and Jarna (Rautakoski) Claassen, with friends in Congo.

Gordon Claasssen, ca. 1986

Karen McCabe-Juhnke

A child at the Mennonite-run daycare center in Bogotá, Colombia, 1995.

Peter Rempel, 1998

Sasha Denikin, daughter of Sergei and Lena, in Ukraine. COM supports the Denikins in their church planting ministries.

Abe and Hanna (Vogt) Rempel, 1995

A children's classroom at the mission at Samachique, Mexico.

97

Bruno Bergen, 1991

A child at the Anahuac Church, Mexico.

Peter Kehler, 1981

Chasing after "threshing cows" in India.

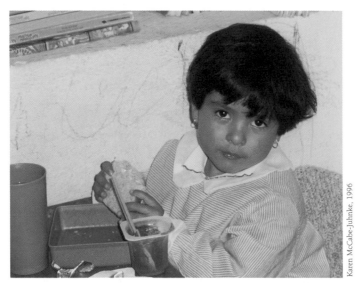

Karen McCabe-Juhnke, 1996

Lunchtime at school in Mexico City.

Herta Funk, 1986

Kindergarten in China.

98

Children of the Hakata Mennonite Church in Fukuoka, Japan.

Stephanie, daughter of Rudy and Sharon (Andres) Dirks, and her friend Doreenie, granddaughter of the family with whom the Dirks family did their "village live-in" in Botswana.

Bruno Bergen, 1986

Boys in N'Dorola, Burkina Faso.

Zeze, neighbor girl of Gordon and Jarna (Rautakoski) Claassen, in Mbuji Mayi, Congo.

Gordon Claassen, 1990

John Bohn

Village baby on mother's back, the most common way of carrying young children in Lesotho.

A COUPLE'S FIRST GIFT

The Liaos were too poor to take their infant son to a doctor but, as Christians, they trusted in the power of God. They asked God to heal their son, and dedicated him to the Lord to be a preacher. The baby was healed, and the Liaos confirmed their vow to God by naming their son Cheng-to, which means "preach the Word," "bring the message," or more literally, "to sow the Word (of God)."

From a young age, Liao Cheng-to was conscious of the meaning of his given name. As a youth he accepted Christ, dedicated his life to serve the church, and gave himself the name Titus. He entered Central Taiwan Theological Seminary and, as a student, interned in several Mennonite churches in Taichung City. Titus had a reputation as a dynamic, well-prepared preacher. During his final year of seminary, he worked in the Peace Mennonite Church, which then called him their leader.

Six months after graduation, Titus married Hannah, a fellow student, who now serves with him in a team ministry. The day after their marriage, Bert Lobe, director of China Educational Exchange, and missionary Sheldon Sawatzky visited Hannah and Titus in the parsonage. The couple asked many questions about the Christians in China. Before the visitors left, Hannah and Titus conferred privately, and came back with a gift of $40 U.S. for the printing of Bibles in China.

—*Sheldon Sawatzky*

Hannah and Titus Liao.

Erwin Rempel, 1989

101

TRUE DAUGHTER OF ABRAHAM

Chizuko Katakabe, a brilliant high school student, spent one year in the United States. Upon her return to Japan, she often visited my wife and me, to explore the Christian faith and improve her English.

In the aftermath of World War II, Chizuko's widowed mother and six siblings had experienced great poverty. Chizuko faced several major decisions. The family's continuing desperate financial situation could prevent her from going to a university, and that would be a tragic waste of her outstanding academic gifts. She struggled with the issue of faith, seldom easy for Japanese people. Chizuko wanted to do "the will of God," but it was not clear what that was. Together she sought counsel with us from the story of Abraham, who trusted God completely to direct his future course.

Later, in the privacy of her room, Chizuko decided to follow Christ a day at a time, regardless of where he would lead. Shortly thereafter in 1964, I was privileged to baptize her as one of the first members of the Nobeoka Church. Chizuko graduated from the International Christian University in Tokyo, and then worked at the Tokyo office of *Reader's Digest*. She was now able to assist her family financially, and did this with much devotion.

When Chizuko's youngest sister could help with family finances, Chizuko took a three-year teaching assignment in Swaziland with Mennonite Central Committee. Chizuko emerged from the assignment with a wealth of experience, and much more confidence in the use of the English language. From there Chizuko left for England and enrolled in the London Bible College. After graduating from a three-year course, she spent 13 years in a fruitful ministry to the Japanese who lived and worked in London. Many were baptized and became part of the Japanese church there.

When Chizuko's aging mother struggled with failing health, Chizuko returned to Japan to take care of her. She spent many days and nights with her mother, and after an agonizing struggle, God answered Chizuko's prayer of many years. Her mother opened her heart to Christ, bringing great joy to both of them.

Chizuko continues to minister to her mother and family. She now serves as pastor of the congregation at Nobeoka.

—*George Janzen*

Chizuko Katakabe assists Pastor Takeomi Takarabe in Nobeoka.

George Janzen

PEACE IN REAL LIFE

The youth group from the Berna Mennonite Church in Santafé de Bogotá, Colombia, had a wonderful time at the 1996 Mennonite church youth convention in Cachipay. As they prepared to return home, 15 armed soldiers arrived. Fear gripped the group; they had heard there were guerrillas in the area. Now they had to face them.

Missionary Frank Soto Albrecht, who worked with the youth, told the group that the soldiers could be bored and just wanted to visit. A bit more relaxed, the group offered the soldiers soda pop, and conversed with them. The commanding officer accompanied himself on the guitar and sang songs he had composed. The songs spoke about Jesus, how difficult his life was, and how he longed to be at home with his mother. His mood changed as he sang love songs written for former girlfriends.

The group was struck with the paradox of having spent four days talking about peace and non-resistance, and now these last two hours in the presence of men holding weapons that could take a life in a flash.

—*Bryan Moyer Suderman*

Mennonite Youth encounter armed soldiers in Colombia.

Chapter 3

Partnerships in Mission

Brazil, Bolivia, Chile, Argentina, Japan, Korea, Northern Ireland, Hong Kong, Thailand, Germany, Russia, Ukraine

Since the 1980s, partnership has been increasingly a part of the Commission on Overseas Mission fabric. More effective witness has come as COM has banded together with other Mennonite mission organizations to plant churches. Some partnerships are part of the movement toward the integration of the Mennonite Church and the General Conference Mennonite Church. Others emerge from the growing strength of overseas churches that are able to mount their own mission ventures.

Brazil

German-speaking Mennonites from Russia settled in southern Brazil in the 1930s, and established communities and churches in the Witmarsum Colony, the city of Curitiba, and other communities. In 1954 the Mennonite Board of Missions began work among Portuguese-speaking people. COM joined MBM in 1974 in ministries of church planting and leadership training, in partnership with the established Portuguese-speaking Evangelical Mennonite Association (AEM).

Missionary Erwin Rempel (right) passes on responsibilities of executive secretary to Teo Penner, a Brazilian Mennonite.

CEMTE students studying homiletics in Campinas, São Paulo, Brazil, in 1987. Abraao Reis (left) is now serving his second church. Joana Darc (center) feels a call to missions in her life. Carlos Carvalho also is a pastor.

In the early 1990s Congo was going through a political upheaval that created hardship for most Mennonites there. A former AIMM missionary to Congo, then working in Brazil wrote:

"Think of it! Brazilians, many poor, young and old, participating in offerings, gathering and selling used clothes, then sending the proceeds (about $600) through AIMM to Congo for missions. Now that's a story. A model church to follow! Giving out of their poverty, being generous, going beyond their ability."

—*Janet (Sinclair) Plenert*

Laying on hands at the 1979 ordination of Osvaldo and Rivanne Freitas in Goias, Brazil: (l-r) Glenn Musselman, MBM; Erwin Rempel, COM; Humberto Mirando, and Otis Hostetler, MBM.

106

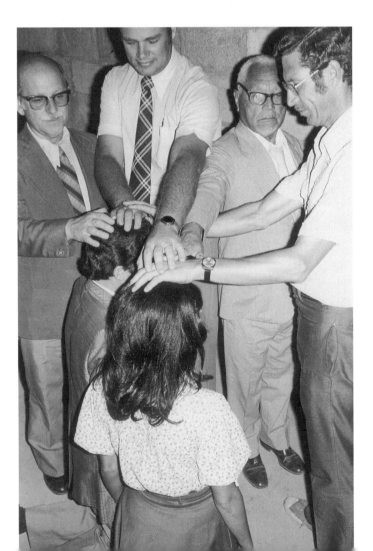

Bolivia

The thought of establishing a Mennonite mission in Bolivia emerged in 1962 out of Mennonite Central Committee's development work. MCC invited COM and MBM to become involved. COM's first workers, Laverne and Harriet (Fischback) Rutschman arrived in 1974. COM, MBM, and other Latin American Mennonites have supported and encouraged the growth of eight Bolivian Mennonite churches. Filled with life, energy, and youth, this small body shows a growing vision for mission, and a desire to train pastors and leaders.

Joyful singing at the Los Tajibos Mennonite Church in Bolivia.

Gathering outside the Evangelical Mennonite Church (The Heart of Christ) during the dedication service in Las Gamas, Bolivia, on January 15, 1989.

Henry W. Dueck, COM missionary (left), talks with faculty and students at the Baptist Theological Seminary at Cochabamba, Bolivia, in 1990.

107

Mission workers Omar and Ester Cortes-Gaibur.

Tina Block Ediger, 1996

Chile

The plight of the poor drew Ester and Omar Cortes-Gaibur back to Chile after their studies in Canada. COM appointed them to build bridges of reconciliation between the rich and poor. In 1998, they opened a home for street children in collaboration with the local municipal government.

Cooks preparing a banquet meal in Chile to raise money for a ministry to prevent family violence.

Argentina

COM's interest in Argentina was heightened when Carmen and Vincent Chen, members of the Fellowship of Mennonite Churches in Taiwan, answered a call to minister to Taiwanese immigrants who had settled in Buenos Aires, Argentina. The Chens are now COM mission associates.

MBM began mission work to the indigenous Toba tribe in the Argentine Chaco in 1943. Through the integration of COM and MBM Latin American programs, COM also became involved in 1997. COM and MBM now relate to the Argentina Mennonite Church as a sister church in the Mennonite World Conference.

COM/MBM missionary Gretchen (Neuenschwander) Kingsley works with women in literacy and Bible study.

Vincent and Carmen Chen, pastors of the Taiwanese Mennonite Church in Buenos Aires, 1992.

109

Charles Shenk

Abba Shalom Community in Korea, 1997.

Chris Mullet Koop

Tokyo, Japan

Since 1951 COM's focus of work in Japan has been on the island of Kyushu while MBM workers were on the island of Hokkaido. Since 1979 they have jointly sponsored a variety of ministries through the Anabaptist Center and guesthouse in Tokyo. In 1997 the center and guesthouse became the work of the Tokyo area churches.

Korea

Yoon-Sik Lee, a man of vision, has led an Anabaptist-oriented community called Abba Shalom Koinonia since 1987. An Anabaptist church called Jesus Village began in 1995 in the nearby city of Chunchon. In 1998 COM, with support from MBM and MCC, appointed workers to assist in the development of an Anabaptist research institute.

Eun Joo Sol preaches at the Jesus Village Church in Chunchon, which seeks to involve the laity. Members are willing to share their resources for the kingdom of God.

Northern Ireland

MBM and MCC have been active in a peace witness in Northern Ireland since 1977. Ten years later, they sent their first workers to serve in inner-city reconciliation in Belfast. COM joined them in 1996 through the joint appointment with MBM of worker David Moser.

Hong Kong

In 1980, COM joined Eastern Mennonite Missions in a church-planting effort begun in Hong Kong in the 1970s. Today the Grace, Agape, and Hope Mennonite churches form the Conference of Mennonite Churches in Hong Kong. Church growth and discipleship is done through cell groups.

Thailand

COM missionaries Pat and Rad (Kounthapanya) Houmphan were seconded to Eastern Mennonite Missions from 1996 to 1999. They work with the Issane people, whose response to the gospel has given birth to the church in the villages in the Det Udom district of Ubon Ratchathani, not far from the Laotian border.

Paul Wing-Sang Wong (front right) listens to the sermon at his commissioning service at the Lok Fu Mennonite Church in Hong Kong.

Pat Houmphan teaching a Bible class in Thailand, 1998.

Jonathan Charles

111

Germany

Thousands of German-speaking immigrants from the former Soviet Union seek a new spiritual life and Christian community in Germany. Though they share a German background, they often encounter rejection and misunderstanding from native Germans. As one of them said, "In Russia we were the Germans; in Germany we are the Russians. We have no homeland."

In 1994 the Mennonite Church in Berlin and MCC invited the Conference of Mennonites in Canada (CMC) to provide workers for a ministry among the immigrants also known as "Aussiedler." CMC provides personnel, while COM and the Mennonite conferences in Germany and the Netherlands help finance this program. CMC workers relate to COM as mission associates.

Church workers from among the Aussiedler are being identified and nurtured to take up the ministry upon the departure of the workers from Canada.

Aussiedler from the former Soviet Union at the arrival camp in Dranse, Eastern Germany, 1993.

Herbert Fransen

Anny (Hildebrandt) Thielmann, Conference of Mennonites in Canada mission worker, with Aussiedler children in the Mennonite Church in Niedergorsdorf, Germany, 1996.

Russia

COM and MCC entered Russia in 1993, appointing workers to build relationships and coordinate material assistance from an office in Moscow. In 1996 and 1997, they were joined by MBMS International (Mennonite Brethren) to establish a witness through an Anabaptist study center in Moscow.

Ukraine

Southern Ukraine was once home to thousands of German-speaking Mennonites. They had initially settled there in response to Catherine the Great's royal invitation in the late eighteenth century. They established prosperous colonies.

During World War II, many Mennonites were deported eastward by the Soviet government or fled westward with the retreating German army. However, a handful remained behind or returned to the Ukraine.

With the new climate of freedom for religious and ethnic groups that followed the breakup of the Soviet Union, some Mennonites gathered in and around Zaporozhye to form a church. Since 1996, COM has supported workers who provide pastoral leadership to the Zaporozhye congregation. COM also sends short-term teachers to the Baptist seminaries and Bible schools in Ukraine. The historic presence of Mennonites in Ukraine, and the role of Mennonite mission workers in the Ukrainian Baptist movement, have given Anabaptist-Mennonite theology an important place in Ukraine's free churches.

Moscow churches.

Peter Rempel

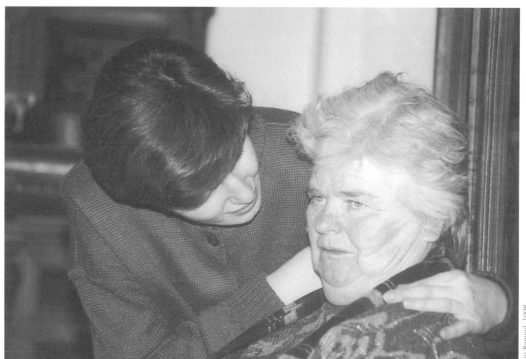

Sergei and Lena Denikin are supported by COM in their church planting ministries in Kherson. Pictured is Lena Denikin with her mother.

Peter Rempel, 1998

113

"I MUST ASK FOR FORGIVENESS"

In 1981, Gary and Ellie (Peters) Loewen began an evangelism and church-planting ministry in Taguatinga, Brazil. Their strategy was to make friends in the community, share their faith, and invite believers into a congregation. One day, when Gary passed Amadeu Coimbra's little house, he noticed him gathering sand, gravel, and concrete blocks to build a small addition. Gary offered to help, but Amadeu was not eager to accept aid from a North American missionary. "What would he know about building in Brazil?" Amadeu thought. But Gary was persistent. Finally, Amadeu agreed to let Gary help.

As the two men worked, they talked. Then they became friends. Their friendship led to conversations about God. A few months later, Amadeu made a decision to become a follower of Jesus.

Amadeu was a linen salesman. He strapped his towels, blankets, tablecloths, and other linens on his bicycle and peddled around the community, selling door-to-door down the dusty streets. Often people couldn't pay the full price in one visit, so Amadeu would return to collect further payments. He began to share his newfound faith as he made his daily rounds. He invited people to come to the new little Mennonite church, and many responded.

Finally, the special day came when Amadeu and his wife Ivonette were to be baptized. The group crowded into a garage for the service. A number of guests were present, including Amadeu's mother and sister, who were not Christians.

Amadeu stood to give his testimony about his faith in Christ, and how Christ had changed his life. He saw his sister sitting in the back of the room and felt a great wound that needed healing. Suddenly, Amadeu stopped. He turned to Pastor Gary and said, "My sister and my mother are here. My sister and I are enemies. We have not spoken for two years. Before I am baptized, I must ask Sirlene for forgiveness." He called Sirlene to come. She rose, thrust her baby into someone else's arms, and climbed through the little folding chairs to meet her brother. Amadeu kissed her. They embraced. They wept. Soon the whole congregation shared their tears as they witnessed this powerful scene of reconciliation.

Amadeu went on to become the pastor of the Taguatinga Mennonite Church which Gary and Ellie Loewen had begun. Amadeu's mother, sister, and brother-in-law became Christians and joined the Mennonite church. Sirlene's husband, Claudio Divino Pereira, became a Mennonite pastor in Brazil.

—Jeannie (Hughes) Zehr,
and Erwin and Angela (Albrecht) Rempel

Amadeu and Ivonete Coimbra, Taguatinga Church, at their ordination on November 24, 1985.

Jeannie (Hughes) Zehr

114

Glendon Klaassen, 1994

*Sirlene Coimbra Pereira (sister to Amadeu Coimbra) and her
husband Claudio Divino Pereira (seated at ends of table) with
COM mission workers Janet (Sinclair) and Steve Plenert.
Claudio pastored the church, which the Plenerts helped nur-
ture and support. In 1998 Claudio and Sirlene moved to
northeast Brazil where he pastored the Lagoa Encantada
Mennonite Church.*

AMBASSADOR IN A WHEELCHAIR

Pong, a sixth-grade dropout and a bodyguard for a house of prostitution, enjoyed getting into fights. He even beat up his father-in-law, which ended his marriage. Pong continued to commit crimes and spent time in Thailand's prison system. Later, while mining for gems, he had an accident that left him paralyzed from the waist down.

Pong's life took a new turn in the mid 1990's when two Eastern Mennonite Missions workers introduced him to Christ. Today, from his wheelchair, Pong is an emerging leader in the Thai Mennonite fellowship. Pong has grown spiritually and in his knowledge of the Bible. Often he goes out alone in his wheelchair to share his faith. Sometimes, especially when people have no interest and reject Pong, he needs patience and courage.

Besides doing evangelism, Pong makes pastoral visits and assists me in teaching the Life Enrichment Course to the seekers. He also is a gifted worship leader and preacher, inspiring people to grow in the Lord.

—*Pat Houmphan*

Pat Houmphan, left, and Pong in Thailand.

Jonathan Charles

LIGHT IN HONG KONG

Hong Kong is an exciting city with tremendous energy, attracting about nine million tourists each year. However, the stress of success takes its toll on the lives of many who live there. Jesus Christ, through his church and his people, is making an impact one person at a time.

Wong Siu-Ling, an immigrant from China, is one such person. Siu-Ling had always been attracted to the Scriptures because, as she put it, "Even we country folk have received an education in Chinese classics and philosophy." She came to faith in Jesus Christ, however, when she was befriended by missionaries Hugh and Janet (Frost) Sprunger.

On June 4, 1989, Siu-Ling and a friend became the first baptized members of the new Hope Mennonite Church, a congregation of working class people. That day, the world was stunned by the massacre of the students in Beijing, China's Tiananmen Square. While the rest of Hong Kong was shell-shocked, Siu-Ling said, "This is a very sad day for China but a very happy day for me." To her, the kingdom of God is greater than the events of the world's nations.

Siu-Ling married Ho Jung, a young man from her village who had become a Christian. Because they were recent immigrants from China, the young couple was unable to find affordable, government-subsidized housing. The neighborhood they moved to was known for its drug dealers and prostitutes.

In this terrible place, Siu-Ling and her family were messengers of Jesus' peace and love. Siu-Ling

(l–r) Hugh Sprunger, Wong Siu-Ling, Jeremiah Choi, and Tim Sprunger.

regularly prayed for the prostitutes, even though she did not know them by name. She helped the elderly in her neighborhood. She washed and combed their hair, cut their nails, cleaned their homes, and washed their windows. Siu-Ling talked to them about the love of Jesus and what it meant to be a Christian. Little Yanyan and Manman, Siu-Ling's daughters, played and talked with the old people. When the neighbors saw Siu-Ling and her daughters, they called out, "Here comes Jesus' little sister!"

One day Ho Jung and Siu-Ling moved into better public housing, and their home became a meeting place where people were loved into God's kingdom. Siu-Ling did not leave Hong Kong in 1997 when it was returned to China. It has been an honor to walk alongside this woman of faith, hope, and love who, without fear, is pledging allegiance to the kingdom of God and lovingly bringing people to meet this life-changing Jesus.

—*George and Tobia (Vandenberg) Veith*

THE POWER OF PEACE

Clemente is a farmer, a church leader, and a man of peace in the community of San Julian, Bolivia. The Lord called him from an immoral life when Mennonite Central Committee volunteers came to Clemente's community to teach in a rural school. They offered adult reading courses, using a modern version of the New Testament as a textbook. Clemente and others learned to read, heard God's good news, and were converted. Soon they were eager students of the Word, were baptized, and formed a small Mennonite congregation.

Tests of faith and life soon came. One of Clemente's neighbors, a German-speaking, conservative Mennonite, believed that Clemente was stealing from him. Clemente visited the neighbor, declared his innocence, and offered to help him search for his missing objects. Clemente, who knew his people and community well, soon discovered some of the items and brought them to his neighbor. With that, the suspicions increased. How could Clemente find the stolen goods if he was not also implicated? Only as Clemente continued to live as a faithful, peaceful neighbor, was confidence slowly restored.

The power of peace became tangible when Clemente and his small congregation built their first meetinghouse. With their own resources and some help from the Commission on Overseas Mission and the Mennonite Board of Missions, they began the project. When the German Mennonite colonists saw the efforts of Clemente and his church members, they offered them the lumber from an old school-house which was to be dismantled. With the additional materials, they were able to build an attractive little church. About 12 persons from this very conservative Mennonite colony, people who normally don't participate in any church service but their own, came to take part in the inauguration service.

—*Henry W. and Helen (Redekop) Dueck*

OUT OF SLAVERY

When we arrived in Germany with our extended family in 1993, we left behind a difficult life in the former Soviet Union.

I, Anganeta Martens, was born in 1928 in Einlage, a village in the district of Zaporozhye, Ukraine. Years of terror at the hands of the Russian Communists ended briefly when the German army occupied Ukraine in 1941. Church life, which had been forbidden for many years, resumed.

This newfound peace was abruptly destroyed, however. The Russian army forced the Germans to retreat, and Mennonite villages were evacuated. With the Russians on our heels, we fled on horse-drawn wagons to Poland. This treacherous journey continued, and in November 1943 we were put on open railway cars that normally carried coal. For six weeks, we headed west across Poland and Silesia until we arrived in Duisburg in the Rheinland. My mother had pneumonia and was sent to a sanitorium in Silesia. We never saw her again. In the meantime, my father found my three siblings. My brother was drafted into the German army when he was 18. We believe he was killed in Hungary.

We worked in Duisburg for one year and then were sent from a refugee camp to Bonn, where we met many Mennonites. The war was raging. The Americans could have saved us but they turned us over to the Russians, who forcefully transported us on railway cattle cars directly to Archangelsk on the Barents Sea in Siberia. Dead tired, and with images of battered, ragged bodies, burned cities, and villages still fresh in our minds, we reached the end of the railroad on November 6, 1944. Dumped in the deep snow in no man's land, we became slaves in the forest labor camps. No church services were allowed. We were spiritually hungry. I lived in this hell for 12 years!

In 1948 I married a Volga German, Edwin Galwas, and six children were born to us. In 1956 conditions improved a little, but suddenly all the Germans were forced to resettle elsewhere. We ended up in Kazakhstan.

Here I found elderly, spiritual people who, through a miracle, had saved their family Bibles and songbooks. Then an old man who had been exiled for five years organized home Bible studies. And so I had the opportunity to study the Word of God. My receptive heart soaked up the good news. I wanted to return to the Mennonite faith of my parents.

After we arrived in Niedergoersdorf, Germany, I found my Mennonite church. Here I received, with joy, Jesus Christ as my personal Savior. My innermost desire was fulfilled on April 21, 1996, when I was baptized, upon confession of my faith, in a Mennonite church.

Since then, joy has filled my heart, and I know I am a child of God. I am able to speak of my past experiences without hatred or bitterness. Joy again filled my soul when my husband Edwin Galwas became a member of our local Mennonite church. I was saddened when he died suddenly on July 17, 1998.

—*Anganeta (Martens) Galwas, via Walter and Anny (Hildebrandt) Thielmann*

Anny (Hildebrandt) Thielmann

Anganeta (Martens) Galwas and her husband Edwin in Germany.

THREE WOMEN ON A DOORSTEP

Three women of the Lagoa Encantada Mennonite Church in Brazil would meet every Thursday afternoon on the front steps of Elizabete da Silva Souza's house: hostess "Bete," an eager new Christian;

Bete selling vegetables at the weekend stall she rents.

Enid (Janzen) Letkeman

Zephinha, an elderly member of the church; and myself. We were an interesting blend of culture, faith background, and personality.

Bete was most interested in studying her Bible. This mysterious treasure book filled her days with hope and promise. From it she received the strength she needed for her struggles—seven children, an alcoholic husband, mounds of laundry, and the daily meals.

Then there was Zephinha, who often delayed her turn to read the Bible by filling her friends in on her personal news, like her latest trip to the doctor. It was Zephinha who gave the gatherings their laughter and humor. One Thursday afternoon when Doña Zephinha was feeling particularly tired, having a hard time concentrating on the text, she looked at me as if to pose a relevant question. She asked, "How come your bottom tooth is like that? Did you break it recently?"

Both Brazilian women also asked thoughtful questions like: "How should I pray? Am I asking God too much when I ask for health, jobs for my grandchildren, and safety for my family?" What a challenge and privilege for me to be the one to explain the very basics of church history and faith to these women!

These women helped and encouraged me, in more ways than they will ever know. As a Christian who has been stumbling along the path for most of my life, I felt most alive and growing in my faith after sitting a while with these women on Doña Bete's front steps.

—*Enid (Janzen) Letkeman*

A GRAIN OF WHEAT, MULTIPLIED

In 1995, a long held dream came true for Izelma de Azevedo of Brazil. The Brazilian Mennonite Church appointed her as a missionary to Macau, a Portuguese colony bordering China. Here, her native Portuguese language would help her relate to the Macanese people.

But first Izelma would study Cantonese in Hong Kong. Jointly sponsored by the Eastern Mennonite Missions board and COM, she considered this assignment a miracle, and her outgoing personality enabled Izelma to quickly develop some basic communication skills.

Just before Easter in 1996, Izelma developed a flu, and missionaries Tim and Suanne (Sprunger) Sprunger rushed her to the hospital for observation. Within 24 hours the Sprungers received a call from the nurse who said Izelma had "gone over the mountain." She had died of a heart attack. Izelma's family in Brazil was crushed at the news and requested that her body be returned to them.

Through a series of divine interventions and with the help of the many Brazilian friends that Izelma had made in Hong Kong, the Sprungers were able to put Izelma's body on the plane a week later. When it finally arrived, a funeral was held immediately, beginning at 11:00 in the evening and lasting until 3:00 in the morning. Thousands attended Izelma's service. Her sister Izaete's tears flowed freely at the funeral. She was sad, but also proud of Izelma's courage and vision. Izelma, who had often

Izelma de Azevedo shortly before her death in 1996.

described herself to Izaete as ugly and poor when she was young, had become an angel of light in the world. Izaete now felt God calling her to Africa as a missionary.

The funeral became a place for many other Brazilians to respond to the call to missions. Izelma was like a grain of wheat which, even as she passed away, sprang into new life.

—*Larry Kehler and Timothy Sprunger*

The family of Julian Espinisa with the Intagliatas' dog, Johnny, in 1992 in Santa Cruz, Bolivia.

A PRACTICAL LESSON IN FAITH

A discipleship class had just ended in our home in Santa Cruz, Bolivia. The subject had been the meaning of faith. The last student to leave was Julian, a bright and inquisitive young man. As he was leaving that night, I realized that our family's dog, Johnny, was missing.

Julian offered to help me look for it. As we combed the streets of the neighborhood, my hopes of finding Johnny grew dim. "Andrew will be heartbroken when he wakes up tomorrow and finds out that Johnny is gone for good," I moaned to Julian.

Julian turned to me and said, "I don't understand why you've given up hope. When you spoke about faith this evening, I was really moved. Where is that faith now?" His words filled me with shame.

The next morning Johnny appeared at our door in the arms of a neighbor who had found the dog a few blocks away.

Julian and his family became dear friends of our family. When we left Bolivia four years later, we gave Johnny to Julian's family.

—*Tig Intagliata*

PEACE IN GRANDPA THIEM'S HOME

Grandpa Thiem and Grandma Khem, husband and wife, had not talked to each other for seven years, though they lived in the same house. Outwardly Grandpa Thiem was seen as a good man by his friends and community. He spent six years in a Buddhist temple for meditation, learning about Buddha's teachings, and practicing a simple way of life. But to the family, he was very proud, unwilling to forgive his wife.

Things changed, however, when Grandma Khem came to faith in Christ. Through a neighbor, she heard about my wife Rad and me. Our "new" religion intrigued Grandma Khem, so she came to the worship services we hosted. Perhaps it would help her arthritis, she thought. After attending the fellowship several times, Grandma Khem decided to take the Life Enrichment course. She gave her life to Christ as her understanding of the Scriptures grew. Grandma Khem knew that even though she was not healed of her arthritis, she had met the real Messiah. Grandma Khem experienced God's help and peace.

Gradually Grandma Khem's attitude toward her husband changed, and she began to talk to him. She was able to forgive him. Grandpa Thiem was utterly amazed at the new person his wife had become.

Seeing the change in Grandma Khem's attitude, Grandpa Thiem began to show interest in the Christian faith. He liked to listen to the native Issane Christian songs that Grandma Khem brought home

Grandpa Thiem (right) assists Pat Houmphan in baptizing Bounme.

from church. When we invited Grandpa Thiem to play the Hai, an Issane musical instrument, during Sunday services, he accepted. Gradually his heart was ready for the gospel and he, too, enrolled in the Life Enrichment course.

At the age of 69, Grandpa Thiem learned that there was a creator God revealed in Jesus. Suddenly he realized that Jesus was the Savior who was prophesied by Buddha a long time ago. Grandpa Thiem understood that Christianity was not a western religion, but that Christ loved and died for the sins of all the people of the world, including his. With this clear understanding of the Christian faith, Grandpa Thiem accepted Christ as Lord and Savior of his life just six months after Grandma Khem. Today, both are reconciled, and there is harmony in the family.

Because Grandpa Thiem is a respected older person in the community, his words and testimony attract others to listen and to learn more about the Christian faith. Through him, some have come to know and accept the Lord.

—*Pat Houmphan*

Yoon-Sik Lee, Anabaptist leader in Korea at the Abba Shalom Koinonia in Hwachon, 1997.

Chris Mullet Koop

ANABAPTISM TAKES ROOT IN SOUTH KOREA

"Who are these Mennonites?" wondered Yoon-Sik Lee, an ordained Presbyterian minister and seminary student. In 1982 he met a former chaplain of the Mennonite Vocational School in Korea, who studied at Eastern Mennonite Seminary in Harrisonburg, Virginia. A year later, Lee and his wife met Burton Yost, a professor from Bluffton College in Ohio who was teaching at Yonsei University in Seoul.

So began Lee's journey with the Anabaptist faith and his search for a biblical understanding of the nature of the church. The journey resulted in his founding of an Anabaptist-based community.

Lee feels Koreans have much to learn from Anabaptism, and hopes real partnership grows between Koreans and North American Mennonites. He wants to see the Anabaptist church in Korea become a key influence in Korea and beyond. One way that happens already is through the large Mission World Building in Seoul. From one inter-church consultation on Anabaptism, this center now hosts a monthly discussion group devoted to Anabaptism in Korea.

—*Thomas Lehman, Chairperson, COM*

NEW LIFE IN THE SLUMS

The story of Izaete (Romão Araujo) Nafziger is typical of children brought up in the many *favelas*, or slums, of Recife, Brazil. To look at Izaete now—married, and for a period of time pastor in the Lagoa Encantada Mennonite Church—you would never suspect how rocky the landscape was at the beginning of her journey.

Izaete was the fifth of eight children whose mother was an alcoholic and whose father worked at odd jobs. She doesn't blame her parents for the way they raised their children. The sadness and the violence that they experienced as "normal" was due to the systems that created and maintained the ongoing reality called poverty.

As a young girl, Izaete was a servant in the home of a rich family. She worked hard all day, then carried home the family's bundle of dirty clothes on her head. Izaete's mother could not cope with the degradation. She drank more and more, and contemplated suicide. No wonder her mother beat the children—she was full of self-hatred and pent-up anger. Even the neighbors were afraid of her!

All of a sudden Izaete's life changed. It happened one evening after a persistent neighbor invited the mother to a huge evangelism campaign near the center of the city. She went, and she returned—transformed! Izaete watched as her mother began to interact with, and actually help, their neighbors. Her mother offered counsel or a cup of rice to those in need. Even Izaete's father gave up his other women and quietly assumed more responsibility for the family.

Izaete's path also became easier and happier. She got involved in the church, teaching children Portuguese Bible choruses. She attended seminary and then worked with a small, new group that no one had ever heard of in Recife: Mennonites.

Izaete helped in the Campos Tabajares Mennonite Church, and visited in the slums around it. As she reflects on the uniqueness of the Mennonite Church in Brazil, she remembers how they treated her initially. Izaete was no longer an object, but someone with value—a friend. There was no hierarchy or totem pole which placed her—a black woman—on the bottom. She had a voice, was listened to, and was accepted for who she was.

What will Izaete's message be as she continues on her path? She will speak of a loving God, a God that helps us cope. A God that walks with us on the paths we take. A God who helps us to be courageous and gracious as we walk the sometimes rough and rocky paths with others.

—*Enid (Janzen) Letkeman*

Carla Reimer, 1994

Pastor Izaete (Romao de Araujo) Nafziger at the church gate in a favela (slum area) in Recife, Brazil..

WE CAME AS STRANGERS, WE LEFT AS BROTHERS AND SISTERS

Raimundo grew up in a family with many brothers and sisters, all of whom were named "Raimundo" or "Raimunda." Poverty in Brazil's northeast prevented Raimundo from going to school. When we met Raimundo, he couldn't even read his own name.

Raimundo and his wife Rita had received and experienced God's grace, and had become faithful members of the Mennonite church. In a land distribution plan, they received a plot of ground in Samambaia, near Brazilia. The couple moved to Samambaia and built a house, but missed being part of the church. To fill that void, they opened their home to a small group for meetings. People from their former church led services on their porch, and a nucleus was formed.

Some months later, we came to help structure the leadership of the church, which meant working with Raimundo. When I first met Raimundo, I could understand virtually nothing he said. My own Portuguese language skills were just starting to come along. Raimundo's gruff manner and quick temper intimidated the new missionary on the block.

Over time, amazing things happened. Raimundo learned to read from his Bible. "A gift from God," he always claimed. Communication between us improved. We had arguments, and then patched them up. I learned humility, and he learned confidence. When Raimundo struggled with doubts about his leadership, I encouraged him. When the church had to make decisions, he showed wisdom and competence.

When we finished our term, we moved out of our house and stayed with Raimundo and Rita, sharing food and fellowship, and saying heartfelt goodbyes. We came as strangers; we left as brothers and sisters.

—*Stephen Plenert*

FREE FROM ALL FEAR

"We've won! We've won!" shouted Elena Loewens, waving her cane as she shuffled down the sidewalk to meet us in Zaporozhye, Ukraine. Elena's harsh life had taken its toll on her body.

We learned to know Elena when she and two other guests joined us for a simple meal which, for Elena, was a feast. She had not seen this much food in a long time. During the meal, Elena told her story.

At the age of two, she lost both parents. The Loewens family took her in. Elena did not know her real name nor date of birth. She remembered little of her adoptive parents. At age 14, due to problems in the home, the Loewens sent Elena away. Destination unknown! Her world changed abruptly.

Elena had never been on a train before. She did not know where she was going. She could not understand the Russian spoken around her. All she knew was Low German. Terrified, frightened, and alone, Elena wept uncontrollably. Finally a stranger asked her, first in Russian, then in German, "Where are you going?"

Still weeping, Elena sobbed, "I don't know." Hearing her story, the stranger advised Elena to get off at Chortitza, where many Mennonites lived. She

did so, arriving at the train station the next morning. No one paid attention to the weeping girl on the curb, where she sat for the next 24 hours. Again, God sent Elena an angel. A kind, German-speaking woman took her home, but for one night only. The kind woman's children were starving, and she had no food to spare. The following day she took Elena to an orphanage, where she worked for room and board for the next two years. They were the happiest years of Elena's life!

A visitor to the orphanage suggested that Elena could earn more working in a factory. Elena was willing to do this but she had no ID card, nor birth certificate. The visitor got the necessary documents for her. With these papers in hand, Elena applied for a job at the factory.

Because she could not read, and her answers to questions did not agree with the documents, Elena was accused of forgery, imprisoned, and then was exiled to Siberia. There she married a Russian man and had a daughter. When they returned to Zaporozhye in the mid-1960s, Elena's husband deserted her. Fortunately, Elena had an apartment and received a pension.

Elena attended a Baptist church in the city, and life took on new meaning. However, her struggles were not over. Her daughter, now grown and

Missionary Susan Kehler and children of the Mennonite church in Zaporozhye, Ukraine, enjoy the advent candles in 1997.

living in Siberia, offered to join her in Zaporozhye. Elena agreed. She would no longer be alone.

However, the daughter did not have her mother's best interests at heart. She forced Elena to live in one room. Two ferocious dogs guarded the apartment, which prevented Elena from leaving her room when left alone during the day. The scars on her body revealed where the dogs had bitten her.

Sitting around the table, we were moved by Elena's story. When the meal was finished, Elena asked for the chicken bones which, she said, would make good dog food!

We were puzzled by her request. Then she explained her announcement on the sidewalk earlier: "We've won. We've won!" She meant that those vicious dogs were now her best friends. No longer was she a prisoner in her own home. From that day on, we gave all our food scraps and bones to Elena to pass on to her new friends.

—*Peter and Susan (Martens) Kehler*

Chapter 4

New Ventures In International Mission

Mexico, Thailand, Chile, Macau, Botswana, Lesotho, South Africa, Burkina Faso, Senegal

The face of missions is changing. Churches established through mission work now reach across cultural and linguistic lines. Missions today is not "we and they" nor "us going to them," but all of us working together. Sharing Christ's love is a global concern. Here are some ways in which the Commission on Overseas Mission is venturing into new territory:

Ethnic Diversity on the COM Team

Today, Commission on Overseas Mission workers represent many ethnic backgrounds and languages. Some immigrants to Canada and the United States in the last decades have returned as mission workers to their homelands, or to other countries. In other cases, international teams have been formed with COM providing support. Some examples:

• Cármen (Gonzales) and Vicente Miñino from the Dominican Republic, co-sponsored by COM/MBM/Franconia Conference, were among the first mission workers from a country other than Canada or the United States, whom COM helped send to a third country—in this case, Mexico.

• Pat and Rad (Kounthapanya) Houmphan, Laotian refugees who settled in North America, now

Cármen (Gonzalez) Miñino prays for a child with mouth problems at Coyoacan Growth Group's children's class in January 1996.

Jeannie (Hughes) Zehr

129

Bible study in the Las Aguilas Mennonite Church in Mexico City, 1992.

Erwin Rempel

Students in class at the Anabaptist Institute in Mexico City, 1996.

Jeannie (Hughes) Zehr

Every Sunday afternoon neighborhood children are invited to the home of George and Tobia (Vandenberg) Veith in Macau, where they are taught Christian songs, hear Bible stories, learn some English, and then play. After the children's time, the missionaries try to visit one of the homes of the children who attended the meeting. Bill Tse, the Macau mission team member from Hong Kong, is seen here with the children in the Veith home.

George Veith, 1998

130

serve their people in Thailand in evangelism, church planting, and discipleship ministries.

- Chileans Ester and Omar Cortes-Gaibur studied in British Columbia, then returned to Chile through COM as Anabaptist resource persons.
- In 1996 an international evangelism and church planting team began work in Macau. With financial support from COM and the Fellowship of Mennonite Churches in Taiwan, workers come from Canada, Hong Kong, and Indonesia.

New Thrusts in Mission

African Independent Churches

When leaders from the African Independent Churches requested help from Mennonite Missions in North America, an exciting era of dialogue and learning dawned. In the 1970s, Africa Inter-Mennonite Mission and Mennonite Central Committee united to form Mennonite Ministries in southern Africa. The African Independent Churches (AICs) appreciated the work of Mennonites. They wanted missionaries to help their church leaders become more established in their Bible knowledge and their ability to bring others to faith in Christ. AIMM agreed to help, but decided that they would not establish Mennonite churches. AIMM began a teaching ministry with the AICs in Lesotho in 1973, in Botswana in 1974, and in Transkei, now part of the Eastern Cape Province of South Africa, in 1982.

African Independent Church leader Samuel Mohono, in his rondavel office in Tabola, Lesotho.

African Independent Church gathering in Lesotho.

Emily Mohono, wife of Samuel, in her home in Tabola, Lesotho.

Mission worker Don Rempel Boschman and Seatla Tlalenyane translate Bible study material into Setswana in 1994.

Church leaders of the Peace Ever Zionist Church in Botswana, 1978.

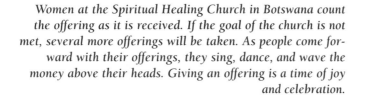

Women at the Spiritual Healing Church in Botswana count the offering as it is received. If the goal of the church is not met, several more offerings will be taken. As people come forward with their offerings, they sing, dance, and wave the money above their heads. Giving an offering is a time of joy and celebration.

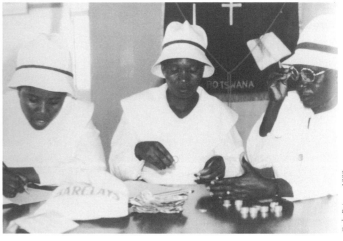

Angela (Albrecht) Rempel

Utlwang Lefoko Church youth choir, 1996, in Botswana.

Gary Isaac

Prophet Mrs. Amanda Mpehla prays for a young woman during a Zionist worship service at the Misty Mount Church in Transkei, South Africa, 1988.

Gary Isaac

New worship garments were dedicated at the January 5, 1992, service of the Misty Mount Church.

Mrs. Bawo reads names of churches to present offerings at a church conference held in 1989 or '90.

Gary Isaac

Jeannie (Hughes) Zehr

Rudy Dirks, missionary, with Bible students Bishop and Mrs. Molosiwa and baby, outside their home in Old Naledi, Botswana, 1998.

133

Ministries in Muslim Countries

Another recent thrust is in predominantly Muslim countries. In 1978 the first Mennonite mission workers arrived in Orodara, Burkina Faso, and two years later, the Mennonite Mission and Church of Burkina Faso was born.

In 1982 linguists Gail Wiebe (Toevs) and Anne Garber (Kompaoré) arrived in Kotoura, a Senufo village in Burkina Faso. They lived among the people to learn their language and culture. Before long, Cheba, the son of the chief, showed

Missionary Dennis Rempel, one of the first COM/AIMM missionaries to arrive in Burkina Faso, teaches a Bible lesson in the Orodara church in 1980.

Musa Barro, eldest chief of the village of Saraba, and his grandson Draman Quattara sit with missionary Donna (Kampen) Entz and her daughter Aisha.

interest in the Christian faith. Two years later, he gave his life to Jesus Christ. Cheba witnessed with joy to others, which led to the formation and growth of a church in that village.

Missionaries and Burkinabe leaders have engaged in church planting, spiritual discipleship, and Bible translation in four languages. Out of this close collaboration, congregations have taken root in Burkina Faso's Mennonite Church.

Another predominantly Muslim country is Senegal. The first team members arrived in 1996 and 1998. Others were to join mid-1999 to do friendship evangelism and church planting in Louga among the Wolof people.

Mission Associates

Joint appointments and programs with other mission agencies, usually Mennonite, have characterized this era of globalization of missions. Through the Commission on Overseas Mission's Mission Associate program, many other countries have been served, including Benin, England, France, Hungary, Israel, and Zimbabwe.

Cheba Traoré with his two wives and children in Burkina Faso: Karija with Emmanuel (left) and Mariam with Daniel (on the right). Standing from l. to r. are Arona, Amidou, and Abi. Since this picture was taken in 1985, three more children were born to this family.

In October 1983, Cheba committed his life to Christ through the efforts of Anne Garber (Kompaoré) and Gail Wiebe (Toevs), COM linguistic missionaries in the village. He was the first known Christian in the entire region. On May 19, 1985, he and four others were baptized. Cheba became a pillar in the church at Kotoura and was respected for his work in the community.

Cheba, unlike other Senufo men, was actively involved in the life and training of his children. In the evenings he, his wives, and children gathered around a kerosene lamp to read God's Word.

In February 1994, at the age of about 36, Cheba died after a very brief illness. The first believer in the area, Cheba left a legacy of 10 years of courageous faith.

In 1995 AIMM sponsored a consultation in Senegal to discuss possible outreach to the Wolof people. Attending this meeting were: (l–r) Kabasele Bantubiabo, Mennonite Church of Congo; Luamba Mbombo, Evangelical Mennonite Church of Congo; Gary Prieb, AIMM executive secretary; and Siaka Traoré, Evangelical Mennonite Church of Burkina Faso.

Missionary Loren Entz with Mennonite church leaders in Kotura, Burkina Faso.

Women ready to take food to the men in the fields, Burkina Faso, 1985.

THE FETISHES HAVE TO GO

Sunday morning's worship service was over. Pastor Ronald Krehbiel shook hands with people as they left the United Church of Maseru in Lesotho, an integrated congregation represented by 28 different Christian denominations and 16 different countries.

Inside the church, Elizabeth Thamae was crying. She said she was a Christian, but continued to go to a witch doctor because her African religion had placed fears in her mind about evil spirits. The rituals she performed at night exhausted her, yet they gave her no peace.

She asked Pastor Ron to come to her house and help destroy all her fetishes—objects she used in performing witchcraft. He agreed to come, and a tremendous burden was lifted from Elizabeth's heart.

The day Ron was to visit her, he became very sick. His wife Cynthia teased him by saying "The devil is after you." When Elizabeth called to make sure Ron was coming, he said he would be right over. However, Ron did not mention his illness.

Ron went to Elizabeth's house. There he was introduced to African fetishes and learned what they are supposed to do. He thought they could simply burn them, but some did not burn. He asked Elizabeth if it was all right for him to take them away and destroy them himself. Relieved, Elizabeth thanked Ron profusely.

The next day Elizabeth called to ask how Ron was. She was still afraid—not for herself, but for what the evil spirits might do to Ron. He assured her that he felt fine, for as soon as he had destroyed the fetishes, his sickness was gone. "How do you feel?" he asked her. "I have never felt better in my whole life," she answered.

—*Ronald and Cynthia (Kirchhofer) Krehbiel*

SOCCER PLAYER SCORES WITH GOD

"You know, the meaning of that song used to pass me by completely, but now I understand," Khux said as he entered the room, bringing me back to consciousness from my mid-afternoon reverie. The lively African melody "*Ke moeti, ke le tseleng* (I am a traveler, on the road)," was playing on my cassette. The song was so familiar to me that I hardly noticed, but for Khux the words carried a deep meaning.

Khux, like many other Botswanan young men his age, failed his primary school. His father's

Khux in action.

Eugene Thieszen

cattle were dying in the drought, so he was running out of options. Finally Khux went to Maun to look for work. With only basic education and no job skill training, he went to work for his cousin, a building contractor. Khux and another young man lived in a ramshackle mud and grass hut. He was barely able to feed himself on his meager wages. Khux's favorite pastime was soccer, and that is what led him to me. I was coaching a local team.

When Khux first came to the practice field, I saw that he was a great player. In fact, he was one of the best goalkeepers I had seen in our area. However, Khux seemed distracted, directionless. When the Ditawana Soccer Club executive met to discuss Khux's difficulties and what could be done about them, I took a leap of faith. Since I had an extra room in my house, I proposed that Khux live with me. I would take responsibility for Khux's support if and when he was out of work. Leswadula, the head of Khux's family, readily agreed and seemed quite relieved that someone was willing to supervise him.

When Khux first attended church with me, he told me that he had no knowledge of the Christian faith. Ten months later, however, Khux decided to center his life in Christ.

Today, even though he still faces many difficulties, Khux has a new outlook, a new stability, and a new energy. Whether he is playing soccer or at work, Khux lives with a refreshing sense of excitement, diligence, and confidence. He knows that he is a traveler on The Road. Destination: the Kingdom.

—*Eugene Thieszen*

STRENGTH TO FORGIVE

It was Maundy Thursday in the village of Tabola, Lesotho. A group of believers gathered to discuss Jesus' words from the cross: "Father forgive them, for they know not what they do." Ntate Motabola, in his late 80s, cleared his throat and told this story:

"In 1970 the election results in Lesotho were declared void by the prime minister because his party lost. The opposition party, which had won the election, then led an unsuccessful coup. This so infuriated the prime minister that he ordered his followers to arrest all who were sympathetic to the attempted coup. Widespread terror followed. Many people fled the country, while others disappeared.

"During this time, late one night, there was a knock on my door. I recognized a young man from our village. The others I didn't know. They ordered me to walk with them to Peka, about five kilometers from my home. When we arrived I recognized others who, like myself, had voted for the opposition party. We were forced to sit on the ground with our legs stretched out in front of us. Men supportive of the prime minister sat on our legs while others beat the bottoms of our feet with sticks. They wanted us to confess what we knew about the coup, or at least give names of people who were involved."

Ntate Motabola became silent. Nobody encouraged him to continue, but he did. "I knew I was innocent, and could only pray." Then he chuckled softly and asked, "Have you ever tried to milk a cow that has wet teats? It doesn't work. One's hands just slip off the teats. And that's how it was with the stick that was beating my feet. It just kept slipping off my feet so that it wasn't very painful.

"All through the night, the beating and questioning continued. Finally at dawn I was released and told to go home. Some of the other men had swellings the size of a big ball on the bottoms of their feet. They couldn't even stand up, let alone think of walking home. I was able to put on my shoes and walk all the way back.

"For some months I avoided the young man from this village who was involved in my torture. Then one day the Lord worked a miracle in my heart, and I was able to forgive him. Instead of trying to avoid my tormentor I could now go out of my way to greet him. I could even go to his home and visit, as is our custom."

But this was not the end of his story. "About 15 years later, the same man who had tortured me was beaten to death by others from a nearby village. They had also suffered at his hand. I searched for his missing body and then sat with his widow. I helped his family dig the grave and bury the man who had tortured me—the man whom I once feared and hated."

When Ntate Motabola finished, he sighed and said, "I think I know how Jesus could forgive as he hung on the cross. The strength to forgive comes only from the Heavenly Father."

—*Tina (Warkentin) Bohn*

John Bohn

Ntate Motabola repairing a bicycle seat in Tabola, Lesotho.

Joseph Mohau Mtebele in front of his business in Qumbu, Transkei.

Gary and Jean (Kliewer) Isaac

 BISHOP'S CONTINUING EDUCATION

Joseph Mtebele lives in Qumbu, a small town nestled in the rolling hills of the Transkei region of South Africa. Qumbu is associated with cattle rustling, faction fighting, violence, and robbery. But Joseph lives there, quietly carrying on his Christian witness as he works in his small carpentry shop on the edge of town.

Since boyhood, Joseph desired to follow Jesus. He joined the Twelve Apostles Church, and later the Christ Gospel of Miracles Church, one of the African Independent Churches. Joseph was baptized in 1970. In 1974 he was ordained a minister, and in 1980 became a bishop of the Christ Gospel of Miracles Church.

In 1982 the Mennonites and Dr. H.L. Pretorius of the Dutch Reformed Church began a Bible-teaching ministry with African Independent Church leaders. Joseph enrolled in 1983. To this day he attends weekend conferences and takes correspondence courses offered by the ministry. Although this is the only formal Bible training he has taken, people have come to trust Joseph as an authority on the Bible. He also serves as chair of the steering committee that coordinates the Bible training.

Joseph's burden for people also includes the needs of the unemployed and impoverished. He is helping to establish a training center designed to provide a better life for his people.

—*Gary and Jean (Kliewer) Isaac*

FINDING GOD ON THE ROAD

Siaka Traoré was the first delegate from Burkina Faso to attend Mennonite World Conference in Strasbourg in 1984.

Siaka came from Burkina Faso, but lived in the Ivory Coast during his youth. He followed the practices of Islam to please his parents. In his teen years, conflict with his father developed. Siaka felt he should be able to worship God freely instead of being forced to.

Siaka got his high school diploma in Ivory Coast. In 1979 he returned to Burkina Faso, where he worked in a sugar factory. Siaka's work pleased the management so much that in eight months, they moved him up four positions. His promotions created resentments among the other workers, who made Siaka's life miserable.

As he sought help through prayer, Siaka felt led to quit his job. He was puzzled and didn't want to accept this answer. But each time Siaka prayed, the same answer came.

For several months he resisted, but Siaka finally put his confidence in God and left his work. Everyone thought Siaka was crazy when he left his job in the city and went back to his home village of Orodara. But it was there, through a catechism booklet, that Siaka first read about Jesus, learned the Lord's Prayer, and repeated it every day. He had not yet met any Christians.

Siaka returned to Ivory Coast to stay with relatives. He hoped that God would find a great job for him. En route Siaka bought a New Testament. During the train trip, he read it all.

In Ivory Coast, Siaka came upon a Christian bookstore, where he bought a complete Bible. He found a Baptist church and was received warmly as a brother. Siaka felt at home and knew this Christian fellowship was what he had been searching for.

He returned once more to Orodara. His search for Christians brought him in contact with COM/AIMM mission workers Loren and Donna (Kampen) Entz. Siaka told them that he wanted to go to school to learn more about the Bible. Some missionaries were not sure of this stranger, but when James Bertsche, AIMM executive secretary visited, he said, "Maybe the Lord has sent him." James encouraged the missionaries to help Siaka.

Siaka was the first person baptized by AIMM missionaries. He attended various Bible schools, studied by correspondence, and got his bachelor's degree. Then, after helping the church in his village for a year, he attended the Protestant seminary in Bangui, Central African Republic.

In 1984 in Strasbourg, France, Siaka became the first Burkina Faso delegate to a Mennonite World Conference. Today, he continues to serve in the emerging Mennonite Church of Burkina Faso.

—*Gail Wiebe Toevs*

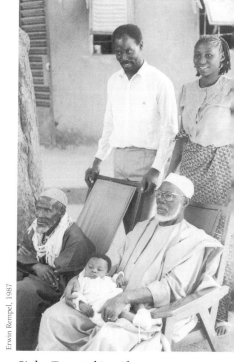

Siaka Traoré, his wife Kienou Claire, and infant son Merveille on the lap of Siaka's father. The father and his friend, left, are both practicing Muslims.

CHOOSING JESUS OVER FAMILY

Word of a new faith spread throughout the Senufo village of Kotoura, Burkina Faso. Children, young people, and an older man made decisions to become Christians.

A Mennonite Church began to form in early March of 1986. An uncle returned from the Ivory Coast and talked his family elders into forcing their Christian boys to leave the faith. The boys, however, remained in good spirits, stuck together, and refused to be swayed. The conflict came to a head on the Thursday before Easter.

Good Friday night we and the Senufo Christians gave an evangelistic presentation in a neighboring village. We got home late and went to sleep as usual. When I got up late the next morning, the boys were at my house with their overnight satchels. They had been kicked out!

Cheba, a church elder, and I asked Cheba's father for advice. He suggested that a delegation request the family to accept their children. That afternoon Cheba, two village leaders, and I met with the family elders.

The meeting quickly intensified, and tempers flared. The elders told Cheba to tell the boys to stop following the Christian way. When Cheba said, "I can't say that," the village leader quickly ushered us out, telling us that the boys should return to their family.

After prayer, Cheba took the boys back. When the older three refused to give in to their elders' pressure, they were told to take the road. The elders did not want to see them again. The younger children were forced to stay in the family and separate themselves from Christianity.

The Christians spent a solemn Easter Sunday together. Early Monday morning, the three young fellows left for Ivory Coast to find work. About a year later, they sent word to the church requesting prayer because they wanted to return to their family. One day they rode in on their bicycles and were allowed to sleep at home. No questions were asked, but tensions remained.

Maadou, one of the boys, longed to be able to show love to his father, but his gestures were refused. Leaving would have been easier, but Maadou stayed, humbly and faithfully serving his family. On November 15, 1987, Maadou was married to his longtime sweetheart, a Christian woman named Traoré Maamou. It was the first Christian wedding to take place in the Kotoura Mennonite Church.

Maadou was active in the church and became one of the youth leaders. He has a gentle, servant spirit, and a love of study and music. In 1991, Maadou was chosen to take further study at a Bible school in Mali in preparation to serve the Senufo church in pastoral leadership.

—*Gail Wiebe Toevs*

Gail Wiebe Toevs

Russ Toevs and Maadou in October 1988.

COMPASSION AFTER-HOURS

In November 1984, I was recovering from cancer surgery at Frere Hospital, East London, South Africa. I was in a large whites-only ward with 19 South African men.

Three days after my surgery, on a Sunday evening after visiting hours, a group of white people entered the ward with a portable organ. They preached; they sang; they made extravagant claims about what would happen to the patients if they adopted their line. These people were loud and impersonal. Not one of them stood at the bedsides of the patients to talk with them or pray for them. They were well-meaning, but when they finally packed up their organ and song books, they left behind turmoil and anger. "Why do they allow these people in here?" asked one patient. "I feel like I've been attacked!" complained another. "Those people make me sick."

Later that Sunday evening, when calm had returned to the ward, I lay in bed with my eyes closed. I heard voices praying in Xhosa, the language of the people I worked with in the South African region of Transkei. Since it was unlikely that black people would be in the ward at that time of night, I assumed that the pain-killing drugs were causing hallucinations, so I kept my eyes closed. The Xhosa prayer continued. Finally I opened my eyes to find two African men kneeling at the foot of my bed.

When they saw that I was awake, they came to me. One of the men was Bishop Tsofelo, the leader of the Apostolic Nazareth Jerusalem Church in Zion, a

man I had known since 1982. He had come from a large meeting of Zionist church leaders in the Transkei, where they had gathered to pray for my recovery from surgery. They had not been satisfied to pray for me at a distance, however; they felt it necessary to choose one

Larry Hills with Bishop Mpehla and his wife at Misty Mount, 1984.

of their members to make the four-hour trip to East London to visit me and pray for me in person.

Bishop Tsofela went first to the large black township of Mdantsane, where he organized an all-night prayer meeting on my behalf before coming to the hospital. For 20 minutes, he and his friend stood by my side. They spoke softly with me; they touched me; they prayed for me. The ward was silent. I saw the patients glancing in our direction. Are they angry? I wondered. What are they thinking, these people who see blacks only as maids and gardeners?

When Bishop Tsofela and his friend left, the ward was silent. I felt at peace. A cough here and a clearing of the throat there broke the silence. Several men began to talk about what they had seen: "I've never seen blacks so confident." "They must really care about you." "They were so different from those other people who were here earlier—they made me angry, but your friends made me feel calm." "I have never seen black people acting that way toward a white person." "That's what Christianity should be."

Several weeks later I asked Bishop Tsofela how he had gained entrance to the hospital on an evening when there were no visiting hours. He said, "First of all, we prayed that the Lord would open the way before us so that we could visit you. When we arrived at the main entrance to the hospital, I dusted off my best Afrikaans and said to the woman sitting at the desk, 'We are Christians, and we want to visit Larry Hills.' She looked surprised, but said that we could enter, although we would have to speak to the head nurse."

"Once again I spoke Afrikaans and said to the nurse, 'Mevrore, are you a Christian?' 'Yes, I am,' she answered. 'Well, if you are a Christian, you will let us in to see Larry Hills, because we want to pray for him.'"

"And there we were, kneeling by your bed, waiting for you to wake up."

—*Larry Hills*

Chapter 5
Toward the Next Century

You have read the stories of Commission on Overseas Mission workers and Mennonite Christians overseas, reflecting God's faithfulness and the Holy Spirit at work during the past 100 years. The twentieth century was the great missionary era for the churches of North America. The overseas mission endeavors of the General Conference Mennonite churches of North America are a microcosm of this worldwide mission advance. From that courageous beginning in India at the turn of the century, the overseas mission movement of the General Conference blossomed into a far-flung enterprise of evangelism, church planting, leadership development, and educational and medical ministries.

From the colonial period through the post-World War II expansion, then an era of partnership, followed by new ventures in the complex world of today—the cycle of missions has come full circle. Churches planted by missions are now mission-sending churches in their own right. But the end is not yet. The task of world missions surges forth unabated until Christ returns.

As the new century dawns, the world we see is vastly different from the one of 1900, when General Conference overseas missions began. The realities of today's world and church present challenges and opportunities scarcely like those of 100

years ago. How the Mennonite churches respond to the new face of missions in the twenty-first century will determine whether or not they survive to write the next centennial edition. These challenging opportunities of the next decades are hinted at by what is happening in missions now.

Local Initiatives. Local churches and regional church conferences desire hands-on, direct communication and involvement in missions. Bypassing the traditional mission agencies, local churches are sending workers to overseas assignments for short- and long-term service. Area conferences are forming their own sending agencies and developing mission programs without reference to the denominational boards. To remain viable in the next century, mission agencies will need to develop new and creative partnerships with the local churches and conferences.

Partnerships. Mission structures, programs, and networks have become complex and confusing. New webs of partnerships are spun in international consortiums with other mission agencies and para-agency groups, with overseas churches, and with ethnic churches in North America. The intricacies of these multiple relationships pose critical personnel placement and funding issues.

Globalization. With the shift in the church's center of gravity from North America and Europe to

145

Waiting to See What Happens Next

When Mrs. Naka became a Christian and was baptized in a Mennonite church, her husband did not support her decision. He strongly objected to her attending services. Now, years later, he no longer sees his wife's faith as a threat, and she comes to church quite freely. An accomplished musician and counselor, she has become an integral part of the Sadowara Christian Mennonite Church in Japan.

Mrs. Naka at the piano, Japan.

Mrs. Naka's father, a devout Buddhist, cannot understand why his daughter does not join him in worship at the family altar. But he knows there is something special about his daughter. He often calls on her for help, even though other children live closer. Mrs. Naka was overjoyed when he asked her to pray for him. She knows God is at work, and waits to see what will happen next.

—*Virginia Claassen*

South America, Africa, and Asia, there has been rapid growth in missions originating from the mature churches of the two-thirds world. Missionaries from the non-Western world will exceed the number of those from the Western world by the year 2000. COM is joining with churches in the two-thirds world for new mission outreach.

Short-term Missions. Limited time commitment is one of the influential values of today's generation. Mission service is viewed as one in a series of meaningful careers in a lifetime. Short-term mission service is the trend, with a smorgasbord of service opportunities offered by mission agencies and local churches. While capitalizing on the value of short-term programs, long-term career workers with in-depth experience in a culture will continue to be indispensable for mission effectiveness.

Prayer Renewal. Christian prayer movements in North American churches are proliferating today. Prayer is concentrated not only on renewal in the churches, but also on intercession for world evangelization. COM has instituted a Prayer Partner Program to involve as many church members as possible in interceding for overseas missions, with many receiving urgent requests by e-mail. Prayer will always be the compelling power in world missions as God works in surprising ways for his redemptive purpose.

Mission is the key to the future. It is the means God uses to bring about the fulfillment of his purposes in history. Only when those purposes are realized will the mission be accomplished, for "This good news of the kingdom will be proclaimed throughout the world, as a testimony to all the nations; and then the end will come" (Matt. 24:14). For the Mennonite churches of North America to proclaim this good news with clarity and power in the next century, we must allow God to remold our thinking for proactive, creative responses as co-workers in God's mission to the world.

—*Sheldon Sawatzky*
COM/MBM Program Administrator, East Asia
COM Interim Executive Secretary, June-October 1998
COM Missionary in Taiwan, 1965-1997

Commission on Overseas Mission
Worker List (with years of service)

Albrecht	Colombia	1993-97
Frank		
Elizabeth Soto		
**Alwine	China	1992-98
Dennette (see Friesen, Todd)		
Andres	India	1951-77
Dorothy (see Giesbrecht, Jacob)		
Andres	Taiwan	1957-62
Esther Mae		
Arn	Taiwan	1981-85
John		
Sarah Kratz		
Arn	Taiwan	1989-92
Kendra		
Assis	Brazil	1987-97
Nilson		
Mary Jane Miller		

Augspurger	Colombia	1967-69
Samuel		
Mary Wyse		
Bachert	Colombia	1948-68
Alice		
Baerg	Japan	1989-92
James		
Ingrid Reimer		
Baergen	Mexico	1959-61
Rita		
Baergen	Bolivia	1986-90
Rudy		
Helen Janzen		
Banman	Congo	1956-71
Hulda	Mexico	1974,
		1975-76
		1978
Bargen	Colombia	1962-64
Eldon		
Helen Bartel		

NOTE regarding Democratic Republic of Congo: Until 1970, it was known as Belgian Congo. From 1970-97, it was known as Zaire. In 1997, it became Democratic Republic of Congo. In this list, it is simply referred to as "Congo."

COM welcomes corrections to this list. We would like to keep accurate records. Please write:

COM
P.O. Box 347
Newton, KS 67114

Bartel	Taiwan	1970-73
George		
Hilda Loewen		
Bartel	Congo	1958-60
Larry		
Bartel	Mexico	1954-55
Norman		
Mary Giesbrecht		
Bauman	India	1958-63
Albert		
Katherine Kaufman		
Bauman	India	1925-61
Harvey R.		
Ella Garber		
Bauman	India	1959-62,
		1967-70
John		
Ruth Gilliom		
Bauman	India	1954-73
Kenneth		
Mary Gallagher		
Baumgartner	Colombia	1989-92
Michael		
Laura Urwin		
Beachy	Japan	
Jonathan		1988-90
Gloria Hegge (see Hegge, Gloria)		1981-84,
		1986-90
Becker	Japan	1968-70
Frank		
Rachel Senner		
Becker	Colombia	1945-49,
Mary (see Valencia, Hector)		1981-87
Becker	Taiwan	1958-63
Palmer		
Ardys Preheim		

Bergen	Taiwan	1983-85
Bruno		
Wanda Derksen		
Bergen	Congo	1983-85
David		
Bergen	Taiwan	1984-86
Elizabeth		
Bergen	Congo	1986-87
Gertrude		
Bergen	Mexico	1956-69
Menno		
Esther Klassen		
Bergen	Burkina Faso	1990-
Phil		
Carol Kliewer		
Bergen	Congo	1985-88
	Senegal	1996-
Richard		
Adela Sawatzky		
Bergen	Former	1993-96
Walter	Sov. Union	
Janet Dyck		
Bergmann	India	1964-69
Nettie		
Birkey	Congo	1923-60
Erma		
Block	India	1961-63
Tina		
Block	India	1976-79
William		
Dolores Friesen		
Boehr	China	
Peter J.		1915-37,
		1947-51
Jennie Gottschall		1915-36
Frieda Sprunger (see Sprunger, Frieda)		1921-37,
		1947-51

148

Boehr	Taiwan	
Richard		1962-71
Lena Peters (see Peters, Lena)		1955-71
Boese	Congo	1984-93
Glen		
Phyllis Thomas		
Bohn		
John	Lesotho	1978-93
Tina Warkentin	Belgian Congo/	1964-75
(see Warkentin, Tina)	Zaire	
Lesotho		1978-93
Boldt	Mexico	1948-49
Cornie		
Born	Taiwan	1983-84
Frank		
Boschman	Botswana	
Don		1985-92,
Kathleen Rempel		1992-97
		1992-97
Boschman	Taiwan	1955-93
Martha (see Vandenberg, J.H. Han)		
Boschman	Japan	1951-71
Paul		
LaVerne Linscheid		
Brandt	Mexico	1976-79
Kornelius Edwin		
Anne Peters		
Braun	India	1908-17
Anna P.		
Braun	Congo	1970-72
Henry		
Sara Jo Lehman		
Braun	Congo	1986-88
Lois		
Braun	Taiwan	1976-78
Wesley		
Catherine Gerber		

Briggs	Congo	1984-92
Maurice		
Joyce Suran		
Brown	China	1911-49
Henry J.		
Maria Miller		
Brown	Taiwan	1960-91
Roland		
Sophie Schmidt		
Brubaker-Zehr	Colombia	1989-95
Scott		
Mary		
***Buhler**	Brazil	1983-92,
		1997-
Abe		
Chris Gingerich		
Buhler	Taiwan	1988-91
Timothy		
Cindy Derksen		
Buhr	Taiwan	1960-63
Martin		
Buller	Congo	1981-83
Charles		
Buller	Congo	1966-89
Herman		
Ruth Lehman		
Buller	Congo	1951-88
Peter		
Gladys Klassen		
Burkhalter	India	1947-90
Edward H.		
Ramoth Lowe		
Burkhalter	India	1917-59
Martha		
Burkhalter	India	
Noah		1919-20
Adah Good (see Wenger, Paul A.)		1919-52

Burkhard	India	1924-31
Mary		
Busenitz	Lesotho	1973-76
Allen		
Marabeth Loewens		
Butler	Japan	1977-80
Stanley		
Camp	Burkina Faso	1997-98
Ron		
Gloria		
Campbell	Congo	1981-84
James		
Cheryl Leroy		
Canetta	Taiwan	1989-90
Rachel		
Chase	Colombia	1991
Jennifer		
Chen	Argentina	1991-94
Vincent		
Carmen		
Claassen	India	1945-75
Curt		
Olga Schultz		
Claassen	Congo	1955
David		
Claassen	Taiwan	1970-73
Elwin		
LaVonne Enns		
Claassen	Colombia	1969-71
Eugene		
Doreen Flaming		
Claassen	Congo	
Gordon		1976-79, 1983-94
Jarna Rautakoski		1983-94
Claassen	Colombia	1971-76
Mark		
Lillian Jacobson		

Claassen	Taiwan	1969
Milton		
LaVonda Buller		
Claassen	Uruguay	1964-72
Sara Ann		
Claassen	Japan	1959-00
Virginia		
***Cortes-Gaibur**	Chile	1996-
Omar		
Ester Concha		
Couillard	Lesotho	1990-91
Troy		
Catherine Schmitz		
Cressman	India	1947-82
Leona M.		
Dahl	India	1964-67
Alfred		
Bertha Martin		
Daku	Brazil	1981-90
Ron		
Marlene Klassen		
Davis	China	1938-41
Etta R.		
de Azevedo	Macau	1995-96
Izelma		
de Brun	Lesotho	1983-86
Harlan		
Claire Becker		
Derksen	Japan	1954-99
Peter		
Mary Klassen		
Derksen	Congo	1976-99
Richard		
Marilyn Carter		
Derksen	Japan	1983-98
William		

Dester	India	1927-57
Herbert		
Hilda Reusser		
Dick	Congo	1975-78,
		1990-94
Delbert		
Susan Mast		
Dick	Congo	1946-81
Elmer		
Esther Quiring		
Dick	Taiwan	1970
Jacob A.		
Dick	Japan	1983-86
Janet		
Dick	Congo	1972-76
LaVerna		
Dirks	Congo	1963-72,
		1982-94
Henry		
Tina Weier		
Dirks	China	1939-45
Marvin		
Frieda Albrecht		
Dirks	Taiwan	1968-83
Otto		
Elaine Ross		
Dirks	Botswana	1996-
Rudy		
Sharon Andres		
Dueck	Japan	1964-67
Agnes		
Dueck	Ukraine	1998-
Cliff		
Dueck	Paraguay	1956-68
	Mexico	1982-89
Henry T.		
Helga Helen Driedger		

Dueck	Uruguay	1969-82
	Bolivia	1985-92
	Latin Am-short	1993, 94,
		1995, 97,
		1998-99
Henry W.		
Alice Helen Redekop		
Dueck	India	1964-66
John		
Winnifred Pauls		
Dueck	Mexico	1963-77
Margaret		
Dueck	Mexico	1980-85
Marvin		
Audrey Heinrichs		
Dueck	Paraguay	1984-86,
		1996-98
Paul		
Linda Winter		
Duerksen	India	1926-55
Jacob R.		
Christina Harder		
Duerksen	India	1956-69
Joseph		
Mary Lou Franz		
Duerksen	India	1948-54,
Marie		1957-63
Dyck	Japan	1953-92
Anna		
Dyck	Botswana	1975-85
		1996
B. Harry		
Lois Riehl		
Dyck	Mexico	1946-48
Frank		
Dyck	Paraguay	1953-68
Frank		
Anne Regehr		

151

Dyck	Thailand	1967-71
Gerald		
Edith Fagerbourg		
Dyck	Paraguay	1967-70
Hans		
Bertha Schmidt		
Dyck	Taiwan	1968-71
Margaret	Mexico	1977-87
Dyck	India	1956-70
Paul I.		
Lois Mae Bartel		
Dyck	Mexico	1962-72
Phillip		
Lora Klassen		
Dyck	Congo	1956-58
Sarah		
Ediger	Japan	
Ferdinand		1953-83
Viola Duerksen (see Voth, Stanley)		1953-83, 1993-94
Ediger	Colombia	1965-74, 1979-83
George		
Margaret Voght		
Ediger	Congo	1971-72
Salomon		
LaVina Gaeddert		
Ediger	Congo	1971-73 1974
Sam		
Betty Regehr		
Elias	India	1991
Jake		
Lillian		
Enns	Lesotho	1995-99
Bill		
Betty Giesbrecht		

Enns	Colombia	1976-81
Erdman		
Linda Rempel		
Enns	Congo	
Frank J.		1926-61, 1966-69
Agnes Neufeld		1926-61
Enns	Colombia	1992-94
Lisa		
Enns	Taiwan	1970-73
Madeleine	China	1985-87
*****Enomoto**	Japan	1998-
Kazuhiro		
Lois Janzen		
Ens	Mexico	1970-71
Annele		
Ens	Mexico	1955-93
Helen		
Ens	Brazil	1964-66
	Mexico	1966-82
Henry G.		
Sara Zacharias		
Entz	Burkina Faso	1989-93
Elena		
Entz	Burkina Faso	1977-
Loren		
Donna Kampen		
Entz	Congo	1949-76
Samuel		
Leona Enns		
Enz	India	1980
Jake		
Epp	Mexico	1975-83
Aaron		
Betty Schmidt		

Epp	Paraguay	1954-64
	Brazil	1965-73
Bruno		
Elizabeth Jantzen		
Epp	Taiwan	1972-86,
		1988-91
Carl		
Hilda Schroeder		
Epp	Japan	1973-76
Delvyn		
Lucille Kroeker		
Epp	Japan	1959-62
Dennis		
Epp	Paraguay	1956-58
Henry H.		
Mary Reimer		
Epp	Paraguay	1956-57
	Uruguay	1957-58
Henry P.		
Hilda Penner		
Epp	Brazil	1993-98
Mark		
Gloria Chacón Alfaro		
Epp	Paraguay	1953-56
Mary		
Epp	Congo	1958-88
Mary		
Eshleman	Taiwan	1988-90
Leon		
Dianna Burkey		
Ewert	China	1929-41
August		
Martha Wiens		
Ewert	Congo	
Ralph		1962-72,
		1978
Fern Bartsch		1962-72

Falk	Brazil	1990-97
Dave		
Patricia Dueck		
Falk	Congo	1952-74,
		1982-88
Peter		
Annie Rempel		
Falla	Colombia	1996-
Gamaliel		
Amanda Arango		
Fast	China	1917-41,
Aganetha		1947-49
Fast	Botswana	1989-94
Eric		
Kathleen Harms		
Fast	Taiwan	1966-70
Frieda		
Fehr	Uruguay	
John		1983-88
Maria Kelly		1987-88
Fehr	Mexico	1955-87
Tina		
Fennig	Congo	1981-83
Charles		
Ferris	Japan	1983-86
Perry		
Nancy Sprunger		
Flaming	India	1991-98
Ronald		
Patrice Stucky		
Flickinger	Colombia	1961-62
Calvin		
Siddonia Nickel		
Fountain	Congo	1983-85
Katherine		

153

Frank	India	
Edgar		1937-39
Johanna Schmidt		1929-39
(see Schmidt, Johanna)		
Fransen	Mexico	1972-74
Nicholas		
Tina Martens		
Freed	Colombia	1963-64
Geraldine		
Friesen	Paraguay	1948-50
A.W.		
Margaret Friesen		
Friesen	Paraguay	1997-
Allan		
Maryvel Vacca		
Friesen	Taiwan	
Alvin		1957-76
Ruby Wang		1965-76
Friesen	Mexico	1979-80
Anne		
Friesen	Paraguay	1959-64
B. Theodore		
Margaret Klassen		
Friesen	Mexico	
David		1967-68
Gertrude Peters (see Peters, Gertrude)		1965-68
Friesen	Congo	1982-85
Don		
Norma Klassen		
Friesen	Taiwan	1983-85
Han		
Friesen	Mexico	1957-60
Helen		
Friesen	Mexico	1984-87
Hilda		
Friesen	Botswana	1986-92
Ivan		
Rachel Hilty		

Friesen	Mexico	1979-80
Jakob		
Friesen	Mexico	1954-60
John		
Mary Giesbrecht		
Friesen	Japan	1950-68
Leonore		
Friesen	Mexico	1969
N.N.		
Friesen	Taiwan	1978-87
	Argentina	1996
Philip		
Kim Vu		
Friesen	Congo	1974
Randall G.		
Friesen	Congo	1986-90
Rick		
June Ashton		
Friesen	Taiwan	1986-89
Rudy		
Sue Heide		
Friesen	Mexico	1976-80
Tina		
**Friesen	China	1992-98
Todd		
Dennette Alwine (see Alwine, Dennette)		
Froese	Taiwan	1982-84
Harry		
Mary Ann Penner		
Froese	Mexico	1960-62
Marie		
*Froese	Korea	1998-
Tim		
Karen Klassen		
Froese	Mexico	1986-89
Werner		
Susan Epp		

154

*Frose   Brazil   1990-94,
1998-
    Rudolf
    Elsie Spenst

Funk   India   1906-12
    Annie C.

Funk   China   1983-90
    Herta

Funk   India   1969-75
    Irene

Funk   China   1984-85
    Laura

Gaeddert   Taiwan   1989-91
    Menno
    Jessie Brown

Gale   Taiwan   1986-88
    Laurel

Garber (Kompaoré)   Congo   1975-76
    Anne   Burkina Faso   1982-

**Gerber   China   1999-
    Robert
    Fran

Gerbrandt   Mexico   1986
    Henry
    Susan Giesbrecht

Gerhart   Lesotho   1974-81
    Robert
    Joyce Stradinger

Gerig   Lesotho   1982-84
    Virgil
    Mary Kay Ramseyer

Gering   Taiwan   1961-64
    Gordon

Giesbrecht   India   1952-77
    Jacob
    Dorothy Andres (see Andres, Dorothy) 1951-77

Giesbrecht   Japan   1953-80,
    Martha (see Janzen, George)   1990-94

Gingerich   India   1976-78,
1983-85
    Kermit
    Clydene Jantz

Goering   Japan   1984-87
    Orlando
    Violet Miller

Goering,   China   1919-35
    Samuel J.
    Pauline Miller

Goertz   China   1921-51
    Elizabeth

Graber   Brazil   1982-91
    Dan
    Rose Waltner

Graber   Taiwan   1956-64
    Glen
    June Straite

Graber   Congo   1951-64
    Harold
    Gladys Gjerdevis

Graber   Taiwan   1967-70
    Kenneth
    Ruth Buhler

Graber   Congo   1957-59
    Larry

Graber   India   1962-65
    Richard
    Melita Goerzen

Grasse   Congo   1986-91
    John
    (Hannah) Betty Stover

Groff   Colombia   1968-70
    Lynn

Groot   Congo   1983-86
    Gary
    Maureen Penner

155

Guengerich	Congo	1946-60,
Frieda		1968-75
Guenther	Lesotho	1981-84
Titus		
Karen Loewen		
Güete	Colombia	1996-
Marco		
Sandra García		
Haas	Burkina Faso	1998-
Lillian		
Habegger	China	1918-21
Christine		
Habegger	Colombia	1963-68
Howard		
Marlene Short		
Hanes	Senegal	1998-
James		
Paula Purcell		
Hanson	China	1994-
Todd		
Jeanette Regier		
Harder	Congo	1968-93
Arnold		
Grace Hiebner		
Harder	Taiwan	1973-76
Eloise		
Harder	Paraguay	1949-50
	Uruguay	1956-76
Ernst		
Ruth Ewert		
Harder	Taiwan	1987-88
Helmut		
Irma		
Harder	Burkina Faso	1985-86,
Judith		1987-89
Harder	Colombia	1966-69
Peter		
Claire Landis		

Harder	Mexico	1977, 79,
Sara Lehn		1980
Harder	Burkina Faso	1985-87
Steve		
Judy Dickerson		
Harder	Congo	1951-61,
		1971-73
Waldo		
Abbie Ann Claassen		
Heese	Congo	1959-60
John		
Hegge,	Japan	1981-84,
Gloria		1986-90
(see Beachy, Jonathan)		
Heinrichs	Mexico	1960-78
Jacob		
Gertrude Loewen		
Hiebert	Congo	1963-78,
Elda		1983-91
	Mexico	1980
Hildebrand	Taiwan	1962-79
Shirley		
Hildebrandt	Taiwan	1968-75
Dietrich		
Margaret Spenst		
Hills	South Africa	1982-89
Laurence V.		
Hirschler	Congo	1971-75,
		1981-85
	Taiwan	1977-79
Richard		
(Wanda) Jean Simpson		
**Hochstetler	Brazil	1998-
Otis		
Betty		
**Horst	Argentina	1998-
Willis		
Byrdalene		

Houmphan	Thailand	1996-
Pat		
Rad Kounthapanya		
Huebert	Mexico	
Roderick		1958-60,
		1982
Ida Unruh		1982
Hunsberger	Taiwan	1971-73
Merrill R.		
Mabel Metzger		
Intagliata	Bolivia	1982-91
Stephen (Tig)		
Karen Flueckiger		
Isaac	Paraguay	1958-61
Anna		
Isaac	India	
Ferdinand J.		1921-46
Anna Penner		1921-47
Isaac	South Africa	1986-
Gary		
Jean Kliewer		
Jansen	Japan	1965-68
Arlin		
Ruth Whittaker		
Jantzen	China	1938-45
Albert		
Wilma Lichti		
Jantzen	India	1938-63,
		1968-76
Aron		
Kathryn Louthan		
Jantzen	Congo	1949-53,
		1955-59
John B.		
Ann Dyck		
Jantzen	India	1947-68,
		1976-83
Lubin		
Mathilda Mueller		

Janzen	Congo	1967-70,
		1976-80
Anita		
Janzen	Mexico	1950-56
B.H.		
Catherine Janzen		
Janzen	Botswana	1985-88
Garry		
Diane Falk		
Janzen	Japan	
George		1959-80,
		1990-94
Martha Giesbrecht		1953-80,
(see Giesbrecht, Martha)		1990-94
Janzen	India	1960-64,
		1969-74
	Nepal	1986-90
Homer		
Margaret Janzen		
Janzen	Congo	1957-59
John M.		
Janzen	India	1964-65
Loretta		
Johnson	China	1996-
Daryl		
Juhnke	China	1987-88
James		
Anna Kreider		
Kagele	Colombia	1967-69
Jerry		
Judy Friesen		
Kambs	Japan	1970-71
Ethel		
Kauffman	Taiwan	1970-80
Lloyd		
Esther Nickel Deckert		

157

Kauffman	Taiwan	1980-83
Robert		
Mary Fisher		
Kaufman	China	1917-31
Edmund G.		
Hazel Dester		
Kaufman	Congo	1955-56
Larry		
Keeney	Taiwan	1977-79
Lois		
Kehler		
Peter	Taiwan	1959-75,
		1991-93
	Ukraine	1996-97
Lydia Pankratz	Taiwan	1959-75
Susan Martens	Taiwan	1957-80,
(see Martens, Susan)		1991-93
	Ukraine	1996-97
Keidel	Congo	1951-81
Levi		
Eudene King		
Keiser	Colombia	1948-62
Arthur		
Helen Morrow		
**Kingsley	Argentina	1997-
Keith		
Gretchen Neuenschwander		
**Kipfer	Bolivia	1997-
Margrit		
Klaassen	Colombia	1959-77
Glendon		
Reitha Kaufman		
Klaassen	Congo	1964-77
John		
Olga Unruh		
*Klassen	Colombia	1997-
Bonnie		

Klassen	Mexico	1979-80
Florence		
Klassen	India	1947-50
Gladys		
Klassen	Mexico	1980
H.T.		
Clara		
Klassen	Mexico	1959-60
Rita		
Kliewer	Japan	1976-80
Henry		
Nellie Krause		
Kliewer	Japan	1967-70
Ray		
Loralee Weinbrenner		
Kornelsen	India	1948-86
Helen		
Krause	Congo	1978-83
John		
Leona Bergen		
Krause	China	1992-94
Pete		
Krause	Taiwan	1968-69
Roland		
Marjorie Vogt		
Kraybill	Taiwan	1967
Willard		
Krehbiel	Taiwan	1973-75
Beth Anne		
Krehbiel	Congo	1976-78
Jean		
Krehbiel	Lesotho	1978-79
Ronald		
Cynthia Kirchhofer		
Kroeker	China	1987-89
George		
Renata Dyck		

Kroeker	India	1900-09
John F.		
Susie Hirschler		
Kroeker	England	1990-92
Mark		
Kuehny	India	1921-37
Clara L.		
Kuyf	China	1936-42,
Wilhelmina		1948-51
**Lantz	China	1998-
June		
Larson	Botswana	1981-94
Jonathan		
Mary Kay Burkhalter		
Lehman	Taiwan	1975-77
Cynthia		
Lehman	India	1960-63,
		1977-79
Jim R.		
Hilda Hirschler		
Lehman	India	1921-37
Loretta		
Lehman	India	1947-67
	Taiwan	1977-80
Melva		
Lehman	China	1918-22
Metta		
Lehman	Japan	1968-71
Terry		
Louise Clemens		
Lehman	Congo	1977-79
Vernon		
Phyllis Lehman		
Letkemann	Bolivia	1975-82
H. David		
Sara Schroeder		

Letkeman	Brazil	1991-95
Melvin		
Enid Janzen		
Leuz	Taiwan	1978-85,
		1992-98
	China	1998-
Christopher		
Lois Gross		
Liechty	Congo	1946-84
Anna V.		
Liechty	Japan	1963-74,
		1977-86
Carl		
Sandra Cook		
Liechty	Congo	1952-73
Irena (see Sprunger, Vernon)		
Liem	Macau	1996-
Shirley		
Lillie	Taiwan	1991-94
Lynne		
Linscheid	Japan	1969-72
Marvin		
Elma Friesen		
Loepp	Japan	1962-64
Franzie		
Dorothy Harms		
Loewen		
David Gary	Brazil	1979-89
Eleanor Peters	Mexico	1973-75
(see Peters, Eleanor)	Brazil	1979-89
Loewen	India	1987
Eleanor		
Loewen	Congo	1972-80
Henry		
Betty Schroeder		
Loewen	Japan	1969-72
Robert		
Anne Konrad		

159

Loganbill	Colombia	1982-84
Marcus		
Cynthia Habegger		
Lohrentz	China	1921-27
Abraham M.		
Marie Wollman		
MacDonald	Taiwan	1979-82
Wayne		
Brenda Loewen		
Mann	Congo	1967-69
Darrell		
Diane Crane		
Marklund	Taiwan	1988-92
Rick		
Ann Morrison		
Marshall	Taiwan	1977-79
Thomas		
Judy Ford		
Martens	China	1996-
Katherine		
Martens	Colombia	1966-68
Larry		
JoAnn Elizabeth		
Martens	Congo	1952-60, 1970-80
Rudolph		
Elvina Neufeld		
Martens	Taiwan	1957-80, 1991-93
	Ukraine	1996-97
Susan (see Kehler, Peter)		
Mathies	Paraguay	1958-81
Eleanor		
Miñino	Mexico	1993-98
Vicente		
Cármen Gonzalez		
**Moser	Northern Ireland	1996-
David		

Moyer	India	1920-56
Samuel T.		
Metta Habegger		
Mullet Koop	Korea	1996-98
Chris		
Laura Mullet		
Myers	Congo	1985-88
Gordon		
Kathryn Graber		
Myers	Colombia	1957-62
Huldah		
Neufeld	Paraguay	1957, 61-62
A.G.		
Neufeld	Mexico	1960-63
Anne		
Neufeld	Uruguay	1960-62
Anne		
Neufeld	Congo	1944-60
George B.		
Justina Wiens		
**Neufeld	Japan	1995-
Gerald		
Neufeld	Burkina Faso	1987-
Gerald J.A.		
Beverly Dueck		
Neufeld	Mexico	1975-78, 1995-96
Jacob		
Ella Klassen		
Neufeld	Taiwan	1977-78
Joseph		
Jeanette		
Neufeld	Uruguay	1960-62
John		
Neufeld	Paraguay	1957, 61-62
Margaret		
Neufeld	Mexico	1957-59
Mary		

160

Neufeld	China	1915-28
Talitha		
Nickel	India	1929-57
Helen E.		
Nickel	Paraguay	1948-50
Jake W.		
Frieda Unger		
Nickel	Colombia	1966-68
Richard		
Bonnie Schmidt		
Nussbaum	Taiwan	1968-72
Karen		
Osborne	Taiwan	1966-68
Philip		
Lorna Hostetler		
Pankratz	Taiwan	1991-92
Doug		
Valerie Heppner		
Pankratz	Taiwan	1956-59
Peter J.		
Theodora Marshchke		
Pankratz	Colombia	1967-69
Steve		
Elizabeth Raid		
Pannabecker	China	1926-41
C.L.		
Lelia Roth		
Pannabecker	China	1923-41
S.F.		
Sylvia Tschantz		
Patkau	Japan	1951-76
Esther		
Pauls	Paraguay	1980-85, 1987-92
Ben		
Patricia Gerber		
Pauls	India	1937-52, 1954-59
Eva		

Pauls	Mexico	1980-81
Jake		
Mary		
Pauls		
John	India	1958-77
	Congo	1980-83
Mary Schrag	India	1952-77
(see Schrag, Mary)	Congo	1980-83
Pauls	Taiwan	1969-73
Mary		
Penner	India	1946-81
Anne		
Penner	China	1984-85
Doug		
Raylene Hinz		
Penner	South Africa	1986
Glenn		
***Penner**	Taiwan	1975-80
	Mongolia	1997-99
Melvin		
Anita Koslowsky		
Penner	India	
Peter A.		1900-41
Elizabeth Dickman		1900-06
Martha Richert		1909-41
Penner	India	1908-49
Peter W.		
Mathilde Ensz		
Peters	Mexico	1956-85
Daniel		
Elma Tiessen		
Peters	Mexico	1973-75
	Brazil	1979-89
Eleanor (see Loewen, David Gary)		
Peters	Mexico	1967
Frank		
Mrs. Peters		

161

Peters	Mexico	1965-68
Gertrude (see Friesen, David)		
Peters	Congo	1959-60
James		
Peters	Japan	1994-95
Leanne		
Peters	Taiwan	1955-71
Lena (see Boehr, Richard)		
Peters	Taiwan	1964-67
Mary		
Peters	Taiwan	1964-67, 1971, 76
Virgil		
Jennie Schmidt		
***Plenert**	Congo	1986-92
	Brazil	1993-
Stephen		
Janet Sinclair		
Poettcker	Taiwan	1973-74
Henry		
Aganetha Baergen		
Preheim	Japan	1966-69
Doyle		
LaDona Thomas		
Quiring	Congo	1936-58, 1961-69
Anna		
Quiring	Congo	1954-79
Betty		
Quiring	Congo	1949-77
Tina		
Ramseyer	Japan	1954-72, 1978-82, 1987-96
Robert		
Alice Ruth Pannabecker		
Ratzlaff	India	1940-77
Harold		
Ruth Regier		

Regier	Congo	1957-60
Arnold		
Elaine Waltner		
Regier	Mexico	1961-63
	Congo	1964-76
	Botswana	1981-85
Fremont		
Sara Janzen		
Regier	Japan	1962-64
Ivan G.		
Anna Preheim		
Regier	Taiwan	1978-79
Lorna		
Regier	China	1926-32, 1940-49
	Paraguay	1950-53
	Taiwan	1955-62
Marie J.		
Regier	Mexico	1975-77
Willard		
Elma Frey		
Reiff	Colombia	1966-68
Bertha Mae		
Reimer	Japan	1957-69
Raymond		
Phyllis Mueller		
Reimer	India	1972-75
Victor		
Mary Thiessen		
Rempel	Mexico	1961-63, 1991-98
Abram		
Johanna Vogt		
Rempel	Taiwan	1983-86
Arthur		
Helen Wiens		

Rempel	Burkina Faso	1978-87
Dennis		
Jeanne Sonke		
Rempel	Mexico	1957-59
Elfrieda		
Rempel	Brazil	1975-82
	Botswana	1994-
Erwin		
Angela Albrecht		
Reusser	Taiwan	1966-69
	Hong Kong	1985-88
Loren		
Peggy Stout		
Riediger	Burkina Faso	1985
Evelyn		
Ries	Congo	1975-84
Dennis		
Shirley Epp		
Roes	Japan	1995-98
Florence		
Roten	Japan	1980
Paul		
Gertrude Wiebe		
Roth	Congo	1954-86
Earl		
Ruth Jantzen		
Roth	Congo	1958-60
Paul		
Rumer	Taiwan	1968-70
Elizabeth		
Rutschman	Colombia	1947-56, 1983-85
	Uruguay	1956-68
	Bolivia	1974-76
	Costa Rica	1977-82, 1986-88
LaVerne		
Harriet Fischbach		

Sawatsky	Japan	1985-88, 1992-
Russell		
Etsuko Yamazaki		
Sawatzky	India	1953-71
Ben		
Leona Friesen		
Sawatzky	Congo	1986-87
Bev		
Sawatzky	Mexico	1980-83
Frank		
Susan Klassen		
Sawatzky	Bolivia	1979-82
Harold		
Valerie Krahn		
Sawatzky	Bolivia	1979-80
Peter G.		
Marge		
Sawatzky	Botswana	1977-88
Ronald		
Sawatzky	Taiwan	1965-97
Sheldon		
Marietta Landis		
Schmidt	India	1927-57
Augusta		
Schmidt	Congo	1980-87
Dennis		
Dianne Smith		
Schmidt	Mexico	1961-63
Donald		
Schmidt	India	1964-70
Edward		
Waldtrout Regier		
Schmidt	India	1945-51
Eleanor		
Schmidt	Mexico	1966-71
Jacob C.		
Lydia Buhler		

163

Schmidt	India	1929-39
Johanna (see Frank, Edgar)		
Schmidt	Congo	1972-74
Olin		
Tillie Nachtigal		
Schmidt	Congo	1969-72
Robert		
Joyce Williams		
Schmucker	Colombia	1988-90
Timothy		
Mary Lou Schwartzentruber		
Schnell	Congo	1932-64
Russell		
Helen Yoder		
Schrag	India	1944-46
Alida		
Schrag	India	1948-53
	Mexico	1955-75
Erwin		
Vera Clocksen	Mexico	1955-75
Schrag	Colombia	1968-70
Leona Jean		
Schrag	Congo	1968-90
Leona May		
Schrag	India	1952-77
Mary (see Pauls, John)	Congo	1980-83
Schrag	India	1973-76
Myron		
Ericka Koop		
Schroeder	India	1952-75
Lorraine		
Schutz	Colombia	1965-70
Julia		
Schwartz	Congo	1942-77
Merle		
Dorothy Bowman		

Senner	Taiwan	1961-66
Edward		
Barbara Beavers		
Senner	Taiwan	1966-76
Ray		
Shirley Leland		
Shelly, Walter	Congo	1968-77
Walter		
Elizabeth Bauman		
**Shenk	Russia	1998-
Phil		
Alice		
Siebert	Taiwan	1964-89
Gladys		
Siebert	Taiwan	1983-84
Joleen		
Siemens	Taiwan	
William		1963-68, 1970-73
Elsie Hiebert		1970-73
Soldner	Colombia	1945-70
Janet	Mexico	1972-76
Sommer	Japan	1970-74, 1989-90, 1992-93
John		
Sharon Wiebe		
Soong	Hong Kong	1987-88
Winfred		
Jean		
Souder	Colombia	1963-66
Daniel		
Dale Myers		
Sprunger	Colombia	1968-70
Barton		
Judith Beitler		

Sprunger	Congo	1958-72
Charles		
Geraldine Reiff		
Sprunger	China	1921-35,
Frieda (see Boehr, Peter J.)		1947-51
Sprunger	Taiwan	1954-78
	Hong Kong	1980-94
Hugh		
Janet Frost		
Sprunger	Taiwan	1981-83
Kent V.		
Sprunger	Colombia	1971-74
Lewis		
Judith Stucky		
Sprunger	Mexico	1976-78
Marsha		
Sprunger	Hong Kong	1981-98
	Asia	1998-
Timothy		
Suanne Sprunger		
Sprunger	Congo	
Vernon		1931-59,
		1961-73
Lilly Bachman		1931-59
Irena Liechty (see Liechty, Irena)		1952-73
Sprunger	Japan	1964-92
Walter Frederic		
Sara Ellen Hostetler		
Sprunger	Congo	1964-74
Wilmer		
Kenlyn Augsburger		
Steider	Taiwan	1966-69,
Kenneth		1974-93
Steiner	India	1913-24
Ezra B.		
Elizabeth Geiger		

Steury	Colombia	1970-72
Clinton		
Nedra Brookmeyer		
Stoesz	Burkina Faso	1993-95
David		
Elvera		
Stolifer	Taiwan	1969-74
Albert		
Lois Unruh		
Stolifer	Taiwan	1984-90
Lois Unruh		
Stucky	Colombia	1945-65,
		1973-87
Gerald		
Mary Hope Wood		
Stucky	Colombia	1992-95
Timothy		
Luzdy Rodriguez		
Stucky	Mexico	1958-61
Willard		
Marjorie Olsen		
Suckau	India	1909-28
Cornelius H.		
Lulu Johnson		
Suderman	Colombia	1993-96
Bryan		
Julie Moyer		
Suderman	Paraguay	1978-81
David		
Alice Claassen		
Suderman	Colombia	1993-94
Derek		
Suderman	Bolivia	1980-86
	Colombia	1988-96
Robert (Jack)		
Irene Penner		

*Suderman	Taiwan	1985-88
	China	1998-
Rod		
Kathi Regier		
Swora	Burkina Faso	1985-90
Mathew		
Rebecca Jackson		
Teichroeb	Paraguay	1964-66
Abram		
Tina Olfert		
Teichroew	Japan	1969-71
Allen		
Kathryn Gaeddert		
Thiessen	India	1952-74
Arthur		
Jeannette Martig		
Thiessen	Japan	1952-86
Bernard		
Ruby Siebert		
Thiessen	Congo	1960-61
Bernhard		
Thiessen	Botswana	1991-98
Erica		
Thiessen	India	1921-49
John		
Elizabeth Wiens		
Thieszen	Botswana	1992-
Eugene		
Thompson	Taiwan	1981-86
Arnold		
Marjorie Wright		
Toevs	Burkina Faso	
Russell		1986-91
Gail Wiebe (see Wiebe, Gail)		1981-91
Toews	India	1984-87
Francis		
Margaret Claassen		

Toews	Congo	1936-40
Henry		
Mary Wiens		
Toews	Mexico	1966-71
Richard		
Betty Janzen		
Tschetter	Colombia	1971-73
Larry		
Edith Hofer		
Unger	Taiwan	1978-80
Ivan		
Marge Zacharias		
Unrau	Botswana	1978-86
Henry		
Naomi Zacharias		
Unrau	Ukraine	1998-
Jake		
Dorothy Klassen		
Unrau	India	1965-66,
		1970-73
Walter		
Ruth Baughman		
Unruh	Congo	1968-87
Donovan		
Naomi Reimer		
Unruh	Mexico	1958-60
Esther		
Unruh	Congo	1990-91
Janinne		
Unruh	Congo	1958-60
Larry		
Unruh	Congo	1931-36
Rudolph		
Unruh	Congo	1946-60,
Selma		1963-65

Unruh	Japan	1951-66
	Taiwan	1978-89
Verney		
Belva Waltner		
Unruh	India	1948-53
Willard		
Selma Dick		
Unruh	India	1928-39
William F.		
Pauline Schmidt		
Valencia	Colombia	
Hector		1981-87
Mary Becker (see Becker, Mary)		1945-49,
		1981-87
Vandenberg	Taiwan	
J.H. (Han)		1957-93
Martha Boschman		1955-93
(see Boschman, Martha)		
Veith	Hong Kong	1991-95
	Macau	1996-
George		
Tobia Vandenberg		
Voran	Japan	1951-71,
		1978-87,
		1994-95
Peter		
Lois Geiger		
Voth	Colombia	1996
John		
Carolyn Harder		
Voth	Japan	
Stanley		1993-94
Viola Duerksen Ediger		1953-83,
(see Ediger, Ferdinand)		1993-94

Voth	China	1919-39,
		1948-50
	Japan	1951-55
	Taiwan	1955-58
William C.		
Matilda Kliewer		
Wade	Taiwan	1988-90
	Hong Kong	1996-
Andrew		
Susan Herzog		
Waltner	Lesotho	1984-91
Harris		
Christine Duerksen		
Waltner	China	1994-95
Melissa		
Waltner	India	1939-56
Orlando		
Vernelle Schroeder		
Waltner	India	1966-69
Robert		
Barbara Burdette		
Warkentin	Mexico	1969-72
Dietrich		
Katie Janzen		
Warkentin	Mexico	1969
Elizabeth		
Warkentin	Mexico	1957-58
Margaret		
Warkentin	Paraguay	1958-62
Mary		
Warkentin	Congo	1964-75
Tina (see Bohn, John)	Lesotho	1978-93
Wenger	India	
Paul A.		1923-52
Adah Good Burkhalter		1919-52
(see Burkhalter, Noah)		

Wiebe	India	1994-95, 1996, 97
Ben		
Patti Mann		
Wiebe	India	1951-64
Esther		
Wiebe	Burkina Faso	1981-91
Gail (see Toevs, Russell)		
Wiebe	Japan	1982-85
James		
Lorna Regier		
Wiebe	Colombia	1966-77
John		
Elma Giesbrecht		
Wiens	Taiwan	1966-67
Esther		
Wiens	Colombia	1985-86
Gordon		
LeAnna		
Wiens	Japan	1990-93, 1996-98
Greta		
Wiens	India	1965-73
J. Wendell		
Norma Bachman		
Wiens	India	1906-37
Peter J.		
Agnes Harder		
Willms	Taiwan	1957-91
Helen		
Willms	Mexico	1960-62, 1968
Margaret		
Wilson	Colombia	1975-77
Larry		
Lydia Jane Krabill		
Wuethrich	China	1940-45, 1947-49
Lester		
Agnes Harder		

Wyse	Colombia	1995-96
Jason		
Wyse	Colombia	1963-64
Rosemary	Uruguay	1964, 67-69
	India	1986
Yoder	Congo	1950-52
Ernest		
Yoder	Congo	1982-85
James		
Linda Bertsche		
Yoder	Congo	1935-50
Roy		
Bessie Burns		
Yoder	Colombia	1953-93
Vernelle		
Yost	Taiwan	1975-76
	India	1981
	Korea	1983-84
Burton		
Elnore Rosenberger		
Yost	China	1984-85
Peter		
Zacharias	Paraguay	1968-70
Frank		
Mary Anne Ens		
Zacharias	Botswana	1985-86
James		
Leanne Derksen		
Zerger	Colombia	1967-69
John		
Sandra Schrag		
Zook	Congo	1955-77
John		
Jeanne Pierson		
Zweiacher	Mexico	1957-58
Clifton		

168

Bibliography

Bertsche, Jim. *CIM/AIMM: A Story of Vision, Commitment and Grace*. Fairway Press, 1998.

Block, Tina. "P.A. Penner, The Champa Sahib-JI." Research paper presented to the Department of History, Bethel College, 1965.

Brown, H.J. *Chips of Experiences*.

Brown, H.J. *The General Conference China Mennonite Mission*. 1940.

Brown, Mrs. H.J. *Praise The Lord*. Freeman, S. Dak.: Pine Hill Printery, 1963.

Juhnke, James C. *A People of Mission*. Newton, Kan.: Faith & Life Press, 1979.

Keidel, Levi O. *War To Be One*. Grand Rapids, Mich.: The Zondervan Corporation, 1977.

Kreider, Robert, ed. *James Liu and Stephen Wang: Christians True in China*. Newton, Kan.: Faith & Life Press, 1988.

Moyer, Rev. S.T. *With Christ on the Edge of the Jungles*. Jubbulpore, C.P., India: Mission Press, 1941.

Moyer, Samuel T. *They Heard the Call*. Newton, Kan.: Faith & Life Press, 1970.

Pannabecker, Samuel Floyd. *Open Doors: A History of the General Conference Mennonite Church*. Newton, Kan.: Faith and Life Press, 1975.

Ratzlaff, Mrs. Harold, ed. *Fellowship in the Gospel India: 1900-1950*. Newton, Kan.: The Mennonite Publication Office.

Unrau, Ruth. *A Time to Bind and a Time to Loose*. Newton, Kan.: Commission on Overseas Mission, 1996.

Voth, Matilda K. *Clear Shining After Rain*. North Newton, Kan.: Mennonite Press, 1980.

Other Sources:

AIMM Messenger, numerous volumes
COM Directory 1996–1998
Directory of Mennonite Missions 1998-1999

Chapter 5

*I*ndex

174

175